# WHO THE HELL ARE YOU?

**ISBN:** 9798878222587

**Imprint:** Independently published

Copyright 2023, Anthony Austen

All views expressed in this book are those of the author and are not intended for use as a definitive guide. This work is owned in full by the primary author, Anthony Austen. No part of this publication may be reproduced or transmitted in any form whatsoever without the written permission of Anthony Austen: anthonyausten@mail.com

 This book was produced in collaboration with Write Business Results Limited. For more information on their business book and marketing services, please visit www.writebusinessresults.com or contact the team via info@writebusinessresults.com.

# WHO THE HELL ARE YOU?

Understand Yourself.
Find Your Purpose.
Live A Better Life.

**ANT AUSTEN**

# ACKNOWLEDGEMENTS

Writing a book has been a thoroughly enjoyable process, but there's just no way I would have done it without the help of Write Business Results. Thank you to Georgia Kirke and all of her team; in particular, thank you to Ivan Meakins and Katherine Lewis for their advice and input.

Special thanks to Ann Bowditch for taking time out of her busy schedule to read the manuscript and write the foreword to my book.

Thank you to all of my friends, mentors, colleagues, football coaches, relatives and work colleagues because you have all taught me something very valuable that led me to writing this book.

And lastly, thank you to my wife Katie, my son Ryan and my daughter Lilly for all of your love, support and inspiration.

*I dedicate this book
to all of the good and bad people
who have crossed my path
because you have all taught me
valuable lessons.*

# CONTENTS

Foreword ................................................................. 11
Preface .................................................................... 13
Introduction ........................................................... 19

Chapter 1: You Are Limitless ........................................... 35
Chapter 2: You Are Time ................................................. 65
Chapter 3: You Are Electric ............................................. 83
Chapter 4: You Are Subconscious ................................. 105
Chapter 5: You Are Habitual ......................................... 125
Chapter 6: You Are Unbelievable ................................. 147
Chapter 7: You Are Insensitive ..................................... 169
Chapter 8: You Are Blessed ........................................... 189
Chapter 9: You Are Under Construction ..................... 207
Chapter 10: You Are One Act Away ............................ 225

Conclusion ........................................................... 245
About the author ................................................. 250

# FOREWORD

To change our world, we must make changes ourselves. So often these changes start with the way we think and how we do things. Ant makes it clear in this book that your destiny lies with you. You have everything you need to be successful and, as you read through each chapter, you will begin to appreciate how you can make success a reality rather than an unfulfilled wish.

The author provides many personal examples of how he used to see himself and his life in a more negative light before he started the process of self-awareness and change. He explains how your beliefs hold you back but also that those beliefs can change. He reminds you to focus on what you actually want.

Ant has done a lot of personal development work and he shares that with you with easy-to-follow techniques. He is open about his old negative thought patterns. However, he is working proof of his methods and he is on that journey with you. Ant also knows when to seek help elsewhere and gives you direction should you wish to follow his lead on this.

One thing the author makes clear is that it is not enough to merely read this book and nod along agreeing with the content – to truly benefit, you need to follow the techniques. Commitment reaps rewards. He really wants you to do well. You will feel him on that journey with you. You will hear him whisper in your ear as you begin your own process to not just find out who the hell you are but also to work towards who you want to be.

The author helps you reprogram your thinking to have that self-belief but also to look deeper at yourself. When you start to become more self-aware, you are able to appreciate where you hold yourself back and then take action. The tools, tips and techniques for success are right here in this book. It will feel as if you have a friend by your side, reminding you to keep going and really wanting you to do well.

I personally know Ant and I can assure you, he is the person you want by your side throughout your own passage to success.

**Ann Bowditch**
Therapist and author of *Stresses of Modern Man*,
*The Power of Confidence* and *The Energy of Anxiety*

# PREFACE

It's just dawned on me that even though I'm writing the preface to a book called *Who The Hell Are You?* on 10 October 2023, you're reading it right now thinking, "Ant Austen, who the hell are you?" Which is fair enough. I like to size up the author of the books I'm reading to see if there's any walk to their talk too.

**So, who the hell am I?**
Well, as you're going to find out for yourself by reading this book, the biggest part of my personality is unseen.

What I can tell you is that I'm a person who challenges the status quo and doesn't fall in line without asking lots of questions.

I don't have the kind of material things that most people mistakenly see as symbols of success. I don't live in a mansion, drive a Range Rover or have millions in the bank. By living a modest lifestyle and not a lavish one, some might say that I have no right to preach about success.

Which is one of the reasons why I chose to write this book. I want to unpack success and highlight that it's a complex word that comes with lots of moving parts. If I could pick just one thing this book achieves, I want it to stop people from believing that success lies in the attainment of possessions. Why? Because people aren't craving possessions, they're craving meaning. Yet, more and more people seem to feel like failures unless they can one-up their Instagram feed.

**This is dangerous.**
When success is reduced to gold watches and attached to certain types of holiday destinations, the latest iPhone and Louis Vuitton handbags, it builds pressure in the lives of people who haven't got these items and breeds misery in their minds. I've seen this toxic way of thinking tear

families apart and push people to the brink of destruction – even off the edge of a cliff.

While the attainment of nice things and a fat bank balance can make you smile for a minute, they won't make you happy in the long term. Playing this game is dumb because you can't win. This has been said time and time again by all of the people from the past and present who own private yachts, Range Rovers and Ralph Lauren suits. Yet, these material items still seem to cloud people's idea of success and signify the pinnacle of it.

### *Success is happiness* – to me.
You have got to decide what success is to you. It's not a one-size-fits-all type of thing. It's certainly not defined by a balance sheet that shows you own a certain set of assets and liabilities. There isn't a universal list of items that needs to be ticked against your name before you're allowed to feel successful.

No one can stamp you with success. Success is a feeling that lives, breathes and is born through you. It's a feeling that rises and circulates from within.

But that can't happen unless you know what success means to you. Success is a personal thing that's unique and relevant to your wants. It's not to be confused with the "success" on show on your Instagram feed.

A large portion of the world's population have success wrinkled in their minds because they're allowing the outside world to control and influence their thinking. Even though they're blessed with a marvellous mind that knows no limits and thinks in perfect pictures, more and more people are walking around with glum faces not knowing what success means to them. (If this is news to you, don't worry, I'll explain just how limitless your mind is in the coming chapters).

### So, why are so very few people thinking for themselves?
The short answer is that they do not know very much about themselves.

They don't understand the scope to which their mind can alter the course of their life. Never were they made aware that they are a goal-striving machine and that thoughts truly are things. They were not told that a huge part of their personality is spiritual, and the spirit is always seeking fuller expression.

Without knowing you have superpowers in your mind and natural laws of the universe to negotiate, you're going to have this hammer and nail relationship with the world. You'll always be bumping heads with circumstance and burning yourself out trying to force success.

**Here's an idea I've fallen in love with that partially explains success…**

> A person is successful when they know where they are, they know where they're going and they're progressively moving in that direction.

Now, that's a pretty simple idea. I'm sure that most people who have delved into the personal development world have heard this idea before. I bet if you asked a group of these people if they understood the idea, they'd all say yes. And if you asked them if they believed in the idea, they would all say yes. In fact, I think if you kept on asking people, you'd come to the conclusion that only a fool would argue that this idea does not ring any semblance of truth.

**So why would these same people who claim to believe and understand this idea continue to rack up results that would indicate they've never even heard of it?**

Well, I've noticed that most people discount the importance of finding out *where they are* because they're so eager to get OUT of where they are. Instead of pausing for a moment to reflect and take stock of where they are, they'd rather sweep their present situation under the carpet and dive head first into the great promise of tomorrow.

If you've done this, (I know I did) let me tell you – you're missing a trick. You've overlooked the working formula and program that has got you to where you are. The proven program and formula that works with or without your consent.

By avoiding a clear understanding of where you are, you're avoiding confrontation with the skin and bones of the reality loop in which you're spinning.

**A reality loop of your own making.**
I'm sure you've come across people who want to get out of debt without looking at their bank statements, who want to lose body weight without stepping on the scales, or who want to find the perfect mate without taking inventory of themselves.

This is a problem because without knowing where you are, you have no grounding; there's no launchpad from which to move forward. Keeping track of your growth and a record of your progress keeps you convinced to keep going on those days when you feel like quitting. With no starting point to look back at, you can never give yourself a tender loving pat on the back because you won't really know how far you've come.

That's why you see an influx of people flirt with the idea of change by making New Year's Resolutions every year. They're using 1 January as their starting point instead of making a committed internal decision to change. Gym owners know this better than anyone. Gyms are rammed in January, busy in February, not so busy in March, and normal business resumes from April to December. Why? Well, you could put it down to a number of things, but I believe the main reason for people not sticking it out is because they don't see instant results.

**It's clear that we live in a world of instant gratification.**
Instant coffee, instant movie rental, instant shopping. While saving us time, us humans are ever increasingly assuming a sense of entitlement through instant attainment of everything life has on offer. Life has become more confusing for young people because everything of convenience comes to them instantly, but anything worthwhile doesn't instantly fall in their lap.

You can't drop body fat, gain muscle mass or improve your lung capacity in an instant. You can't write a book, build a business, become a millionaire or run a marathon in an instant. All of these things take time. I believe the instant world we live in is stifling one of the amazing higher faculties in the human mind – the will.

So much so, there seems to be an air of scepticism around the principles of positive change. The proven success recipe of human desire mixed in with faith and persistence is all under question just because it doesn't instantly spit out the result.

Instead of making a decision and doing whatever it takes to succeed, a mass of doubters are "giving change a go" to see if the shady self-help advice works for them or not. When the changes don't show up in an instant, people either feel doomed to circumstance or they slip back into the reality loop that took them years to form.

**This is where the "how to do it" vs "how it works" saga comes into play.** When you're shown *how to* do something, someone else is telling you what to do. The trouble with this is that people resist being changed by other people. Even people who want to induce fast change in their own lives run into resistance when it comes to following someone else's suggestions.

By contrast, when a person knows *how it works*, in this case how *they work*, they're more likely to change in a flash because they have decided to do so, not been told to change by someone else.

By developing a clear understanding of where you are, what you are and how you got here, you're then armed with the self-awareness of knowing how you work, which is what you need to get to where you want to go.

**At the end of the day…**
To change your results you have to be willing to change yourself because they're your results. Again, a simple idea that makes sense. But when was the last time you interrogated yourself?

The truth is, none of us are immune. We're all infected with old ideas that are holding us back. Even if you're a seasoned self-development junkie, I bet you've still got some old ideas skulking around in your psyche that aren't doing you any favours.

The good news is that you have the ability to change your present conditioning, and by doing so, you will sprinkle success in all areas of your life. But what's required to change your conditioning won't make sense to you until you understand how it got there in the first place.

Seeing a way forward to get where you want to go is much easier, and you're more likely to believe you can make the journey, when you know how you got here. So, how did you get here?

# INTRODUCTION

Someone else took control of your life the moment you were born.

It may have been your mother, father, grandparent, aunt, uncle or guardian. These people loved you, cared for you and protected you to the best of their ability. They taught you how to survive. They fed you, bathed you, sung you lullabies, read you bedtime stories and much, much more. They passed on everything they knew about life, all in a quest to see you do well.

But there reaches a point where no one is in control of your life any more. There's no one to hold your hand as you cross the road. No one to remind you to brush your teeth. No one to hang your clothes in your wardrobe. You have to fend for yourself.

Naturally, the people who were in control when you were a child loosened the reins as you approached adulthood because you became more and more able and independent. Unlike the wildebeest who is ready to run away from the lions 15 minutes after being born, it takes us humans a number of years to keep all of the lions at bay. When the time comes, you suddenly find yourself standing shoulder to shoulder with all the other adults. Finally, you're in control.

Your moment has come to start living life on your terms – as if it were that easy.

You throw yourself into adult life, feeling optimistic about your prospects. A few years go by and your life hasn't turned out like you thought it would. Life is much harder than you thought it was. You want to be your own person, but you can't and you don't know why.

I can tell you why, although knowing won't provide you with an immediate solution. The reason you're struggling to be your own person is because you're essentially running a program that was, in large part, built by someone else. You're operating with a set of inherited behaviours, beliefs and habits that you adopted from the people who were around you when you were growing up.

This is a problem due to the fact that you want different results to the people who were around you growing up. Not to outshine them, look down on them or because you believe that you're better than them, but because you are different to them. You think different thoughts, you feel different emotions and you want different things. Your wants, dreams and desires are unique to you, so you need to know who you are.

That's where this book comes in. Its purpose is to give you the knowledge that everything you need to succeed is already inside of you. I want to dispel the myth that only a small number of people are born with the traits to succeed and the majority of people are not. As you read the following chapters, you'll learn you really can reconnect with your unshakeable childlike confidence and slip out of the straitjacket of adult life – you really can start betting on yourself. You have so much more going for you than you're even aware of yet. Trust me.

### The pitfalls of "success"

I've written this book because I want to prevent you from spending your life chasing "success" only to realise years later that you've paid a heavy price along the way.

My Dad got me my first job when I was 15 years of age. I was over the moon and I'll always be grateful that he used his connections to land me my first job, but I'd be lying if I told you that going to work for a removals company was ever my decision.

It also wouldn't be true to say that eight years later I started my own moving company because I wanted to. This decision was a knock-on effect of the initial decision that I would work for a removals company – a decision I did not solely make. As a result of starting at the bottom of a removals company and rising through the ranks, starting my own removals company seemed like the next logical step, so I took it.

Once the honeymoon dust of starting a new business had

settled, I soon cottoned on to the fact that I no longer worked 9am to 5pm because I now worked non-stop. I didn't have 20 days of paid holiday a year because I now had zero. I thought my business would give me more freedom, but I found the opposite to be true.

All of the structure I had in my life fell away not because I had a lot to learn in business (even though I did), but because I had married a business model that traded time for money. In order to earn more money, I'd need to give more of my time away. Those were the facts. But I went into business because I thought it would give me more free time.

If I had known back then that my ultimate desire was to own a great business that got more profitable without me having to be there, I wouldn't have handcuffed myself to a time for money industry that I wasn't overly passionate about for over 20 years.

In a sense, I ended up with a successful business that offered a service not because I wanted to, but because I knew how to deliver it well enough to make a living out of it. I'd spent years honing my moving skills and I wanted to own a moving company that delivered the best moving service possible. In return, I expected to receive the kind of compensation that would give me time and geographical freedom.

I live on an island that's 31 miles in total coastline, so my choice of business was not compatible with my ultimate desires. Its reach and customer base was somewhat limited by a small demographic. I was essentially running in circles through operating a service business on a rock.

How did I become an owner of the wrong business model for me at 23 years of age? Through my desire, faith and persistence that was fuelled by believing, "If you work hard, success is guaranteed." This is another fixed idea that I did not originate or ever examine. I just took it onboard and started working hard on whatever was put in front of me. I never once questioned it because I had heard it from someone who I thought couldn't possibly be wrong.

So there I was, the successful businessman who everyone in earshot would say was doing well for himself. Yet, the better I made my business, the worse I made my health. The more happy I made my customers, the more unhappy I made myself and my family. The more energy I spent on customers, the less energy I had to spend with friends.

The Saturday that turned my life around was my son's sixth birthday. While he was blowing the candles out on his cake and lapping up the cheers and applause that followed, I was pushing a moving team to the brink of exhaustion in a sweaty office to please a couple of impatient corporate bigwigs.

They expected the entire contents of their office to be packed up, manhandled and relocated in a flash. Piling pressure on me to hurry my team to get all of the desks in place so the IT guys could get the business back online – anyone would have thought a dying person had been unplugged from life support.

I remember getting home at 6pm on that Saturday feeling run down and drained. My son told me about his birthday and I didn't really have the energy to listen. It was as if I wasn't bothered – which couldn't have been further from the truth.

This was when I realised that I had spilt blood, sweat and tears climbing to the top of a ladder that was leant against the wrong wall. The saying, "be careful what you wish for" suddenly made a whole lot of sense to me.

The time had come for me to start thinking for myself instead of following the footsteps and the advice I'd gotten from other people who meant well, but did me no favours.

High-performing CEOs, business owners and senior leaders have always been a danger to themselves. Willing to sacrifice their sleep, their children's nativity plays and their wedding anniversary celebrations if it means making progress towards success. They want to level up their health, wealth and relationships to benefit their families, but they often find themselves lopsided in these areas, which makes them feel emotionally out of balance. They mean well, but the price they pay for success is often irreversible and not worth it. However, they only learn this when it's too late. It all becomes clear after they get divorced, their grown-up children have no time for them or they have a heart attack or a stroke.

On reflection, they realise that innocent people got hurt because they were chasing the wrong things. They thought they were getting closer to making themselves and their loved ones happy, but they weren't. And who gave them the idea that they were on the right track? Themselves or someone else?

In this book, you're going to learn how to take full control of your life by understanding how your conscious and subconscious mind works. Early in my own self-development journey, I kept running into this recurring theme – we become what we think about. I didn't understand.

If the main thing separating rich people from poor people was a mindset, how so?

If rich people were rich because they were money conscious and poor people were poor because they were poverty conscious, how does a person develop a consciousness? And can a person change their state of consciousness?

I was curious. These questions lead me into a continuous study into the workings of the mind, and how a person can become what they think about.

Once I found out that all of the ideas planted in my subconscious had already manifested into results, I knew that I had a proven template to follow to plant new ideas in my subconscious that also would manifest into results. The results I wanted.

I could now start thinking hard on how a purposeful life would look for me because I now knew what I had to do to live it. I suddenly dismissed the idea that I was a static person who had already had his lot in life. I had full faith that all I had to do was plant my ideal life in my subconscious mind and it would manifest into me living a life of purpose and meaning.

I had a new-found optimism that I could reconnect with who I actually am and start living my life by personal design. My design. And I was right, because I learned that I'm blessed with creative superpowers, and so are you.

You're also blessed with all of these creative faculties in your mind that are responsible for all of the material things you see in the world, and you'll learn how we're all subject to universal laws that are exact.

I'll also share how you can improve your relationship with the world by bringing yourself into harmony with these universal laws that are nailed down and absolute. The laws I talk about here are not an exhaustive list – there are others. I've simply covered the ones I believe are most useful for you.

The reason why understanding the universal laws is paramount to your success is so you know exactly how things in the world *do* happen and how things *can* happen. When you know how things do happen and how things can happen, you're able to construct strategies and place yourself on a road map that leads to happier outcomes. It also makes the journey a more pleasant trip.

Let's start with an easy one.

*The Law of Gravity* is pretty clear, right? Knowing not to walk out of the third-storey window or jump out of a flying plane without a parachute is excellent information.

My son learned the Law of Gravity very early in life. At 18 months old, he decided to climb out of his cot. Over the guard rails he went, falling head first onto the wooden floor. You might be thinking that's a pretty harsh lesson for a toddler to experience, and you'd be right, but the laws take no mercy just because you don't know how they work.

Not me, you or anyone can negotiate and make a middle-of-the-road deal with these laws. They're set in stone. They won't wrap around your little finger nor will they bow down to your flippant commands, take pity on you or soften the blow when you fall flat on your face because of your ignorance. The universal laws are a set of impersonal rules that play no favourites and will not budge or bend their ways to the politics of what's considered as playing fair and not playing fair.

The wisest thing you can do is study the laws and shape your commands to work with them, rather than against them. I'm sure anyone would rather create a free flow with these universal resources instead of working themselves to the bone and banging their head against a brick wall trying to force things over the line.

When you're using the laws, you're guaranteed to speed up your progression because you've placed yourself on the greased railroad to what you seek. Working with the laws is like strolling down the moving walkway at the airport. You'll make more progress in less time with less effort because your direction has been set in motion, which means reaching the destination is inevitable.

*The Law of Polarity* cites that everything has an opposite.

Hot/Cold. Tasty/Bland. Loud/Quiet. Night/Day. Wet/Dry. Up/Down.

The big one we're going to focus on in this book is "Good/Bad" because I feel people lock themselves into a negative polarity by the constant use of the type of language and thought habits that keep them where they are and convince them to never aim any higher.

They lock themselves into a prison of their own making by the compound stacking of their unconscious responses to minor everyday altercations that they can easily change.

According to the Law of Polarity, nothing bad can happen in life unless there's something good about it. Therefore, there's no such thing as "no good". That may surprise you, but it's a fact. There'll be times when you will have to look hard at an unpleasant situation to find what's good about it, but there will always be some element of a bad situation that can be turned to advantage.

Thankfully, you're blessed with the privilege of choice. You always get to choose which polarity of every experience you're going to side with. You've got the ability to think negatively or positively, but you're not capable of thinking both negatively and positively at the same time. If you dismiss this, try it right now and see if you don't agree with me.

Personally, I've likened the practice of finding the good to a form of mind control that's similar to how an automatic pilot brings an aeroplane back on route when some unexpected turbulence knocks it off course.

By using the Law of Polarity on a daily basis, you can pull your focus away from the negative and back on to the positive expression of all situations, and by doing so, eventually you form a thought habit that constantly keeps you feeling optimistic and upbeat about life.

When you feel good, you're working with the Law of Vibration.

*The Law of Vibration* tells us that everything is energy that's vibrating at a certain frequency.

Water, steam and ice are all a form of the same energy that's vibrating at different frequencies. It's the same with wood, paper and cardboard and no different when it comes to human excitement, anxiety and elation.

The Law of Vibration even considers the love between two people as a form of energy that's vibrating at the same frequency in two bodies. So, if you have a spouse, business partner or a team to lead, you want to be sure you're all on the same frequency so you're working with each other, rather than against each other.

In Chapter 3, You Are Electric, you'll learn how you're a form of energy that's vibrating at a certain frequency, and how you can change the level of your vibration with some simple practices.

Understanding the Law of Vibration gives you the assurance that what you want is nothing more than a form of energy that vibrates on a different frequency than you. All you have to do is bring your level of vibration on to the same frequency as the thing you want in order to get it.

By working with the Law of Vibration, you're priming yourself to work in conjunction with the razzle-dazzle law so many know and so few fully grasp… The Law of Attraction.

*The Law of Attraction* says that *like attracts like* – as in the energy you emit is the energy you attract.

## Introduction

Yes, *energy flows where attention goes*, so positive thoughts do bring positive results and negative thoughts bring negative results. However, this does not mean that the one and only thing you have to do is think about something and you'll get it.

The Law of Attraction is very clear in saying you can only attract to you what is in harmony with you.

If you *hate* poverty more than you *love* prosperity, you're in harmony with poverty, and you're going to attract more of it. You may have written down a goal to save money, but if you're always thinking about spending money, you're not going to save money.

When the unaware person doesn't see an instant result in their outside world, they back away from using the Law of Attraction to their purposeful advantage and sit on the sidelines of their life. They may even start believing that some people are just born blessed, some are not, and they're one of the people who are not so they won't attempt to do anything of any great consequence because the odds are stacked against them.

I suggest these people improve their lives by enjoying getting super-specific with their "perfect world" scenarios. They should have a play with the Law of Assumption.

***The Law of Assumption*** is the principle that what we assume to be true will become true for us.

Visualisation plays a huge part here. In closing your eyes and using the creative powers of your mind to flash up crystal clear images of everything you want, you then assume it to be true by thinking, feeling and acting as if your desires were fulfilled.

Wallis D. Wattles, in his book *The Science of Getting Rich*,[1] says this is the hardest work a person can do, and that a person should devote

---

[1] Wattles, W.D. (2007) *The Science of Getting Rich: The Proven Mental Program to a Life of Wealth*. National Geographic Books.

as much free time as possible doing it. Continued use of this law gives your subconscious mind some heartfelt food for thought, and since it has no concept of time or reality, it will get working right away and want to make the things you assume you to be true to actually be true.

*The Law of Compensation* states you will be compensated in direct proportion to what you do, your ability to do it, and the difficulty to replace you.

If you want to earn a lot of money, the need for what you do must be very high. Your ability to do it must exceed others in your field, and the difficulty in replacing you must be one hell of a challenge.

A tremendous amount of people are making far less money than they're capable of purely because the money they do earn is reliant on their physical presence. Once a person is able to deliver service without their physical presence, the more service they can render, and the more money they can earn.

*The Law of Cause and Effect* states that whatever you do or say will cause some effect.

My friend's Dad telling us 10-year-old boys that we could forget the idea of becoming professional footballers unless we could kick the ball well with our weak foot had quite the *effect* on me.

It *caused* me to spend hours and hours kicking a football against a wall with my weak foot.

The *effect* of the hours of practice is that now I don't have a weak foot when it comes to kicking a football.

This has *caused* many people to make the inaccurate remark that I'm a natural two-footed football player. The real reason is because of the Law of Cause and Effect.

I can kick a football equally well with both feet because I've kicked the football thousands of times with each foot.

*How to* get good at something is through repetition. *How repetition works* is because of the Law of Cause and Effect.

All of the success gurus say, "Repetition is mastery." Very few tell you why.

Think about it. Everything you practise *causes* some *effect*. Practising the same thing twice *causes* twice the *effect*. Practising the same thing ten times *causes* ten times the *effect*.

As Bruce Lee, martial artist, Hollywood film star and the founder of the martial arts philosophy Jeet Kune Do, put it, "I fear not the man who has practiced 10,000 kicks once. I fear the man who has practiced one kick 10,000 times."[2]

## How to get the most from this book

The best way to utilise this book is by reading it again and again to cement the ideas in your mind. I suggest you handwrite a debrief of each chapter in your own words so you can make sense of what it all means to you. This will spark ideas of your own that could very well lead you to the success that you seek. If you're anything like me, you'll ignore that instruction and just start reading the book. That's OK. Just make a commitment to reread it and take the action suggested. Repetition is mastery — there's a good reason why the best teachers return to ideas again and again, because it's how we, as humans, learn best.

Repeating an encounter fuses it into your awareness. Just think of how many times someone restated or revisited a concept you thought you had already learned, but then it yielded a deeper meaning in the new context and you thought, "OK, now I understand it." Yet, our instant world encourages us to cover more content in less time to train ourselves quickly instead of slowing down to fully grasp what we're learning in the present. In short, repetition seems to be a backward retreat but it's actually the fastest way to take a giant leap forward.

Reading and writing makes an impression on the mind. As surprising as it may sound, the main thing I want you to gain from reading

---

[2] *A quote by Bruce Lee* (no date). https://www.goodreads.com/quotes/96374-i-fear-not-the-man-who-has-practiced-10-000-kicks.

this book again and again is an ever-broadening awareness of your awesome power to change so you can bring an abundance of good into your life. And also so you know that the smartest, most effective thing to do whenever you're facing an outside challenge is to slow down and return to yourself.

It's my opinion that a person with a broad awareness of their awesome power to change holds all the cards to their better future. They're able to duck, dive and shimmy past life's challenges because they're able to pull on the levers of change with absolute faith. It's the awareness that stabilises the faith and overrides the sporadic flickers of fear that want to move in and slow a person down.

The Law of Cause and Effect states that reading this book once will cause a certain amount of awareness in your mind, so if you read it 20 times, you're going to be 20 times more aware of your awesome power to change than someone who just reads it once.

This puts you at a huge advantage compared to someone who reads this book once, memorises a few lines and then moves on to the next book. Someone else may be able to recite some ideas and phrases better than you, but that doesn't mean a thing. A person's understanding of the information they've taken the time to relay so well is relative to their results, not to their words.

I know people who skim-read just for the sake of getting through a load of books, and what I've noticed is that none of the books they read ever seem to get through to them. They end up surrounded by a load of useful knowledge, but that's of no use to them because they haven't taken the time to study the information.

This book will also help you become self-aware, which is foundational for success, as I know from experience. I started a business in 2010 not knowing my limiting beliefs about people, money, marketing, sales, leadership and customers would hold me back. Being brutally honest, I didn't know what limiting beliefs were, let alone know that I had them and that they were responsible for all of my unconscious responses. I thought that moving forward in life came solely down to skill. I didn't know

## Introduction

that I had 23 years of conditioning that made me think, act and feel a certain way.

I thought that all of my problems stemmed from outside challenges and circumstances. Never did I want to consider that it might actually be something to do with me – that the reason I kept running into the same problems was because I was running a program that was coded by my own unaddressed inner conflict. Does that sound familiar? Are you always looking for answers outside yourself rather than turning your focus inwards?

Although we need to examine our past before we can move forward, what I'm trying to say is that you don't have to drag around your past for the rest of your life. You don't have to frogmarch yourself towards someone else's version of success. It's possible that you can be happy, healthy and wealthy without taking blood pressure tablets or signing divorce papers; you can overcome the challenges of the past and design the future you want so you can be free and powerful in the present. You can achieve all of this simply by getting to know yourself better.

So, do yourself a favour right now. Take this moment to galvanise the magnificence that's waiting within you. Grab yourself a pen and a pad and write a debrief of this introduction in your own words. If you're not sure where to start, write down one to three things you didn't know before; alternatively, imagine you are summarising what you've read for someone else. What do you feel compelled to share with them? It will only take five minutes. Get writing and amaze yourself by reading back some thoughts and ideas that you were not aware that you had.

The more you understand yourself, the more you understand other people and your relationship with the world so that life becomes more of a pleasant ride. You'll love the way you spend your days once you've developed the faith to direct all of your thoughts, feelings and actions towards your wants and desires.

Yes, what you do is the cause of your results, but what you do isn't the problem. The problem is what causes you to do what you do, and what causes you to do what you do is your conditioning – the fixed ideas in your subconscious mind that are causing you to act in alignment with them.

Just because you're in the driver's seat doesn't mean you're in control. Think about when you learned to drive and your instructor had their own set of pedals that would override yours. Often our limiting beliefs act like a fearful driving instructor, hitting the brakes when we think we should be accelerating. The only way to prevent that from happening is to show your driving instructor that you've got this – but you can only do that if you know they're in the passenger seat in the first place. Ultimately, our aim is to lose the driving instructor and their second set of controls altogether.

When you acknowledge and confront your limiting beliefs, you're taking full control of your life. You pass your test and can drive on the roads alone.

This is when you can find out what you're made of. Right now though, you have some work to do to uncover who you are and what you're capable of.

Just because you know your name, it doesn't mean you know who you truly are.

> The best part about me is I am not you
>
> **Marshall Mathers (Eminem)**

# YOU ARE LIMITLESS

There are certain things in life that you don't need to know.

Yet, information is being thrown at you from all angles. You're living in a world of information overload that gives you instant access to heaps of knowledge with a click of a button. You just cannot move for the information you literally have at your fingertips. It's all too easy to gorge on all the facts, hacks and stats about this and that for hours on end. You can onboard cutlets of data about nothing in particular which gives you stacks of disposable knowledge, a cluttered mind and leaves you knowing very little about lots of different things.

With free passage to the latest and greatest tips, tricks and conspiracy theories, the average person bundles as much information as they can into their memory, which has them believing that they're well educated. Without meaning to offend or sound blunt, that's a huge reason why they're living an average life at best and why their results are well below the scope of what they could achieve. They're not driving the kind of car they want to drive, not living in the house they want to live in and not going on the type of holidays they want to go on.

The truth is, the average person is not very well educated at all when it comes to getting what they want out of life. Yet, there are so many smart people with all of these degrees, A-levels and important letters after their names who can mesmerise you with their general knowledge. They can pull words from the back of their mind and string together impressive sentences. They can talk a better game than the people who are actually winning. They seem to know all of the answers to life, but they can't get what they want out of life because they don't even know themselves. Did any of that ring true for you? If it did, don't shy away from it – this is true of most of us, myself included before I started on my journey of self-development and inner discovery.

I read all the books, took all the online courses and attended all the seminars in search of an answer or one secret hack that would solve all my problems and have me living my best life, but I didn't know what my best life was because I didn't know myself.

Rather than searching inside and asking myself what I truly wanted, I looked around at my present situation in the outside world and thought the solution was to master what was going on there.

I thought I needed to systematise my current business so that it operated like a well-oiled machine and got more profitable when I wasn't there. This would mean I wouldn't have to fight fires on a continuous basis, which would cut me the slack I thought I needed to be a better parent, husband and friend.

I didn't know it, but I was locked into a negative reality loop of my own making.

If I had slung my thoughts inwards and asked myself what I truly wanted, I'd have called myself out earlier and would have made my life better sooner. I'd have known that I was the owner of a business I wasn't passionate about and that the business model wasn't compatible with the way I wanted to live my life. I'd have known to start making plans to get out of a business that ran me down and tested my patience and integrity on a daily basis.

Instead, I dived into all of the books, courses and seminars in a quest to grow the business I wasn't passionate about, and grow it did. Thanks to the outside knowledge I gained from other people's strategies and my application of it all, business boomed! All my problems were solved, right? Wrong. I was more trapped than ever in a business that butted heads with my values on a daily basis.

My body was beaten, my mind frazzled and my ears were ringing with the words of American life coach Tony Robbins: "Success without fulfilment is the ultimate failure."[3]

Up until that point, I thought life was a struggle for me and my family because I lacked information about the workings of the outside world. Little did I know, it was the inside information I had running around my head that was the cause of all my troubles.

Despite the way school has taught us, loading up on snippets of information about a broad range of subjects is no measure of how educated you are. To read a book once, answer questions from the book, get graded by someone else, and then move on to the next book just isn't going to cut it when it comes to being able to get what you want from life. The best students get high marks based on their memory and how much information they can relay, not for their understanding of how to put themselves in a solid financial position or create a happy household, for example. It's one thing gathering information and developing your memory so you can recite certain answers to win a quiz or to get an A* in an exam. It's a whole different ball game developing your mind so you can draw inner guidance from it and form your own opinions that lead to you living a purposeful life by personal design.

The contents of any book (or audio, online course or seminar) can't possibly be understood by just reading it once, but that's what most of us do. We read a book, listen to an audio, go through an online course and then move on to the next one. That's how we've been taught. When a person does this, they put limits on their potential to take the kind of actions that really make a difference to their lives. This is because they

---

[3] Tony, T. (2018) *Grow & give*. https://www.tonyrobbins.com/leadership-impact/grow-and-give/.

have a limited understanding of what they've learned, which means they can only put half-measured actions into practice and get half-measured results.

When you think about it, students are always answering someone else's questions. They're always seeking acceptance through someone else's way of thinking and, you could even say, are encouraged not to have an opinion of their own. That's why so many people end up nettled in life through the worry about other people's thoughts and what other people might say or think. The unvoiced message that school puts across is that other people's opinions are more important than your own opinions, which is a huge reason why people go about their days with this belief at the forefront of their minds. They're always listening to someone else, falling in line with someone else's rules and forever putting their own wants on hold. They're limiting themselves as a result.

By contrast, an educated person responds to their wants. They're not hopping on and off the various carousels of knowledge in the outside world. Instead, they're thinking for themselves. They choose to hush the outside world by closing their eyes in a quiet, undisturbed space because they know where the questions and answers that they need are. They know that the guidance they need is floating amongst the continuous flow of thoughts that are endlessly coming to them. It's as if they drop into an atmosphere of their own inner thought universe and consult an unseen alternative world for ideas to reason with. By being aware of their boundless power to change that awaits direction in their inside world, an educated person can answer the questions they derive from themselves. They know exactly how to renovate their reality any time they like by using the unseen part of their personality and backing their own judgement. Basically, they know how to get what they want out of life. That's my definition of a well-educated person.

This is the kind of person you have the capacity to be – it's the kind of person I want you to become by reading this book and applying the success habits I share throughout.

The Latin word for "educate" is "educare", which means "to bring or lead out from within". So, learning isn't just about gathering information, it's mainly about inducing, developing and drawing out ideas and intelligence from within – and you have an infinite source of ideas and intelligence from within. If you think not, turn off your thoughts for the day. How did that go? Obviously, you can't stop thoughts coming to you, which, even though a little eerie, is a wonderful thing. It means you can look in the mirror right now and know that whatever life throws at you, you have all the talent, ability and answers that you're ever going to need already inside of you. No debate needed. It's just a matter of drawing it out.

School gives the impression that a person is an empty cup, and the idea is to fill up the cup with general knowledge, but that's not true. That would indicate we're limited beings who should not be encouraged to think for ourselves, that once the cup is full, that's it for us, we're done – we've grown to capacity. The truth is that far from being empty when we start school, we're already full.

So many fantastic books, inspiring life coaches and great achievers are in unanimous agreement that a person becomes what they think about. They've all said that every person possesses a boundless power to change through an invisible power that's greater than themselves and can be tapped into through using the creative faculties of their mind. When mixed with desire, faith and persistence, every person can do anything they set their mind to. But it all starts from within; from the inside world.

## Tapping into your infinite potential

So that means that you and I were born with infinite potential. I'm not limited. You're not limited. And that makes the successful people you admire no different to us. I'm not just saying it for the sake of geeing you up or motivating you. I believe that motivation must come from education. Otherwise motivation melts in the face of resistance like a red-hot Mars bar.

An educated person is motivated by default because they're educated.

They know what to do because they know who they are. They know their energy flows from a higher to lower potential and construct their lives in accordance, and as a result they stay motivated.

In all seriousness, you're a limitless, spiritual being that's living in a physical body. You've been blessed with a mind that has all of these non-physical creative faculties that give you the ability to manifest the life of your dreams, which are…

**Intuition**
**Imagination**
**Reason**
**Will**
**Perception**
**Memory**

These are the creative faculties that separate you from your pets and all other lifeforms, so let's go over them one by one.

### Intuition

Your **intuition** helps you understand something without the need for reasoning. I remember when someone suggested I use my business knowledge to become an online business coach. As I played with the idea, a little inner voice kept telling me, "Don't be a business coach because a person needs something else in place before they can be successful and happy doing business."

I didn't know what that *something else* was that I felt a business person needed in place back then, but my intuition was telling me not to be a business coach. It was steering me away from it and moving me towards my purpose, which is to help people become aware of all the creative powers they have at their disposal so they can live their life by design.

*Example: Leading up to every football match I'm due to play in, I get an intuitive feeling that I'm going to score at least one goal in the game.*

### Imagination

Your **imagination** gives you the ability to form any image in your mind at any time. You can form a detailed picture in your imagination that your eyes haven't seen yet. You can even make a picture no one else's eyes have seen yet, just like Thomas Edison did when he ploughed on through a reported 10,000 failures before he introduced the lightbulb to the world. Today, trillions of eyes have seen the picture that Thomas Edison was seeing in his mind for quite some time.

The great thing about the imagination is that you can make the future the present so you can create and align yourself with ideal circumstances.

This is what all the great athletes do and it's what you should do in whatever area you wish to shine in. It's a way of familiarising yourself with the perfect scenario that hasn't happened yet so you can get yourself ready and stay ready – so you can grasp the moment with both hands when it does happen.

Hollywood movie star Arnold Schwarzenegger said in his Netflix documentary that he won the Mr Olympia bodybuilding contest every night in his imagination long before he actually did. Despite the fact that he was physically lying down in a single bed in his little childhood bedroom in Austria, in his mind, he was in America holding the Mr Olympia trophy up to a crowd who were all chanting, "Arnold! Arnold! Arnold!"

When everything Arnold Schwarzenegger formed in his imagination actually happened in real life five years on from when he started, he knew that, without a shadow of doubt, it was no coincidence. He had stumbled upon visualisation not knowing how powerful it is and not knowing he was working with the Law of Assumption. The laws are impersonal. You don't need to study a law for it to work for you;

you only need to be doing what needs to be done to be working with a law.

Arnold was just doing it because he enjoyed seeing himself as a winner in his imagination. He was doing what some will say is living in cloud cuckoo land or losing touch with reality, but after seeing his private vision play out in real life, he had a firm conviction that visualisation would bring him what he wanted in life.

Little did he know he was doing what all the great books on the mind have taught and what every successful person agrees with – that we become what we think about.

By his own admission, Arnold Schwarzenegger then used his imagination to win Mr Olympia seven times, appear in 40 movies, set up multiple businesses and to become governor of California. As you can see, this is a vast range of success which just shows that one person is not bound to static success in one area.

I'm firmly convinced that I can create anything that I can form in my imagination.

> *Example:* *I use my imagination leading up to the football match by closing my eyes and forming an image of me scoring a certain type of goal.*

## Reason

The gift of **reason** permits you to accept or reject ideas, thoughts and suggestions.

A person who neglects to get a handle on this faculty is a person who will always be controlled by the outside world because they won't be controlling the direction of their thoughts.

I suggest that you take the lead of your reasoning faculty because it reasons both with and/or without your blessing. This means you could end up accepting ideas that shunt you in the wrong direction from your goals simply because you're not minding the door of your mind.

Let's face it, there's always going to be something going on in the outside world that's going to control you if you let it. So, through the conscious use of reason, you can stay in control by taking the time to analyse and size up an idea, thought or suggestion rather than just accepting it by taking someone else's word for it.

You owe it to yourself to be in control of you because no one else has been given the responsibility to live your life for you. You have the full right to kick a thought around in your mind and form your own opinion. When a thought comes to mind or an idea is thrown your way, the question to ask is not, is this right or wrong? The question to ask yourself is, will this idea, thought or suggestion move me closer to my worthy ideals?

If it doesn't, think of something else. If it does, think on. This is the key that ignites the engine of your mind to start thinking about how you can bring the idea to life and forgetting why you can't.

> *Example:* I use my reason faculty to examine the idea and image of what I've made of me scoring a certain type of goal in my imagination by deciding whether this is a positive or negative thought I want to get emotionally involved with. Since it's a positive idea, I accept it by continuing to think about it. Thoughts of why I can't score this type of goal always come to mind. That's OK. I know I have no control over the thoughts I'm given. I also know I do have the control to stop thinking about why I can't and continue thinking about how I can.

## Will

Just by using your **will,** you'll improve your commitment, discipline, attitude and decision making in a flash. Conscious practice helps you concentrate on a certain objective for a sustained period of time so you can develop a laser-like focus that you can beam on to the tasks that make you successful.

Willpower often comes up when someone is trying to kick an addiction or a disempowering habit. It often comes up in these shades of conversation, which is perhaps why the will is a human superpower that's overlooked and stays associated with the negative aspect of life.

Stubbornness is also a negative expression of a person who's strong willed.

Start thinking of the will as positive because it's one of your perfect creative faculties. If you were to ask me what one thing it takes to be successful, my answer would be the will to do it.

> ***Example:*** *I'll hold the image, thought and scene of me scoring a certain type of goal on the screen of my mind to the exclusion of all other thoughts and outside distractions. The longer I do this, the stronger the connection I make with the idea of me scoring a certain type of goal and the more likely it will happen because it's being impressed upon my subconscious.*

## Perception

The magic of **perception** is that you can see things from more than on perspective without the use of your eyes. You can look at things from different angles and take polar-opposite opinions and beliefs over certain situations that prompt you to take different actions that lead to various outcomes. There may be three or four ways to look at one situation, for example. You can zoom in, pan down or get a full panoramic view of the circumstances so you can get the full gist of what's going on before making a decision to proceed or retreat.

You've heard a story from someone who's telling you how their spouse mistreats or disrespects them. They're so convincing that you start to feel for them. Before you know it, you have a little soap opera in your mind that's based on what you think is a fair opinion of something that quite literally cannot help the person in need or advance your life.

A few days later you hear the spouse give their side of the story and your opinion changes because you can now see their point of view. That's called changing your perception. And it's important to understand that there's always more than one way to look at things because we often limit ourselves by how we perceive things. Yet, if we're in the habit of looking at scenarios through a narrow lens instead of using our perception, we're never going to get the full picture and therefore limit our chances of making a wise decision. Being able to change your perspective on an unfavourable image, event, conversation or circumstance acts as a diversion to a more favourable outcome.

Example: As if I'm unpausing a static image on a TV, I mentally press play on the image and turn it into a live scene in my mind and I observe the goal from all angles. I'll see the ball come into my path and watch the ball come off my foot as I kick it towards the goal. I review the entire scene as if through my eyes, the goalkeeper's eyes, from grass level, from sky level, from behind the goal and so on. I do this to broaden my awareness of the idea and to move it into form.

### Memory

Your **memory** allows you to onboard truckloads of data so you can revert back to it and make better decisions in the future. You can dive back into your past to draw wisdom from the bad times or you can simply bathe your consciousness in the good moments. Ultimately, your past informs you and every breath you've ever taken is lodged in your memory.

> *Example: I cast my mind back to my yesterdays and bring up memories of me scoring goals in the past. I then put myself back into those moments and stir up the same emotions that were running through me when I scored those goals. This gives me the real-life emotions that have put me in harmony with scoring*

> *goals in the past, and once I feel them rushing through my system, I'll put my mind back in the new image, reviewing the scene in the first person with those same emotions activated.*

It's never been a secret that you can bring your innermost desires to life through the right use of your mind; it's just that most of us are sceptical about things we can't identify with our physical senses of sight, hearing, smell, taste and touch. When a person doesn't know whether they believe something and don't know where to start, the odds are very high that they'll never try.

And yet, everything you see around you was first just an **intuitive** idea that was formed in someone's **imagination**. Then it was **reasoned** with and held on the screen of the mind through the use of the **will** until the idea moved into a theory. Then it was built into a fact through the persistent use of **perception** and **memory** drawn from the inevitable failures that act as the stepping stones to success.

You don't need to go out and grind, hunt or buy these creative faculties. You're already armed. You're already using them. You're just probably not aware that you're using them through neglect, not aware of what they are, not aware of how they work with the laws of the universe, and not aware of how they've positioned you in the immediate outside world you see around you right now. If you're reading this book it's likely that you don't realise the figure in your bank balance represents how much you know about yourself. Well, you do now.

Multimillionaire, business coach, property investor and multiple business owner, Brad Sugars is a person I consider to be a mentor of mine through his books, board game and online programs.[4] Now, Brad learned all about wealth from Frederick J. Eikerenkoetter II (June 1, 1935 – July 28, 2009), better known as Reverend Ike, a reverend, prosperity teacher and speaker you can find on YouTube who said, "The

---

[4] https://bradsugars.com/

reason the car manufacturers make different cars is for different states of consciousness."[5]

He made the point that to have a lot of money, you need to be money conscious; to be successful, you need to be success conscious, and so if you don't have a well-designed self-image of the person you want to become, you're not conscious of that person, and so you can't have what that person desires.

The money you have in your bank, the shape of your body and the car you drive are all a reflection of your own consciousness. The present size of your consciousness is largely determined by how conscious you are of yourself with regard to your unseen powers.

Wouldn't it be handy if the supercomputer mind that you were born with came with an instruction manual on how to use it? Only by delving into the inner workings of who you are can you gain a thorough understanding of who you are, what you have and how you work so you can put yourself on the road to success.

As you continue to learn more about yourself, you'll cast doubt and worry aside because you'll be moving forward with understanding. It's through understanding yourself that you become attractive to success, because when a person is aware of their strengths, weaknesses, excuses, beliefs and how to change them, that person is able to weather the storms that every success brings. Understanding where your fear is coming from gives you the faith to move towards your worthy ideals because you'll be aware that the only problem you're ever going to have in life is you. But without an understanding of how things can happen for you instead of to you, faith cannot exist.

You simply cannot remain in ignorance if you want to be successful. It doesn't matter how much desire you have to do well in something – as long as you remain in ignorance, you'll always carry a seed of doubt around in your psyche that'll dampen the fire in your belly at every turn.

---

[5] From Brad Sugars' online program *30x Business*

Ignorance is the reason why nothing changes for most people who want things to change.

So many people watch a motivational video on YouTube, jump off the sofa and embark upon the mountain of change with desire in their rucksack, only to soon find themselves on a slippery slope back to reality as they know it. I'll hold my hands up to rolling down that slippery slope on more than one occasion.

Here's why it happens. Ignorance breeds doubt and worry, and ignorant people can only react to doubt and worry by doubting themselves and worrying about what could go wrong. They start losing momentum, the doubt and worry turns into fear, which sets up a bad feeling in their body, and they think, "Is it all worth it?" Soon enough, they've made the decision to give up on changing things so they can get the familiar, safe feeling back in their body. They choose to stick with what they know rather than step out and really bet on themselves. So they remain boxed in and get frustrated as a result. There are a couple of things going on, but the main culprit is ignorance.

It's such a shame because when crippled by indecision, cap in hand with their shoulders slumped, tenacious people with the ferocity to run through brick walls to get what they want reduce themselves to circumstance. They scour for shortcuts and remain on the prowl for an easier way to create the change they want to see. When it dawns on them that there are no shortcuts and their flawed plan bears no fruit, they'll either give it one last shot or throw in the towel and fraternise with the darker side of their nature. What a waste. How dangerous. All due to a lack of understanding.

So, how do you gain understanding? There's only one way: through study.

That's the only way to give ignorance the slip: to permanently remove it from your sleeve. We're all ignorant, by the way – and I'm not saying you have to know everything about everything. When my car breaks down, I don't have a clue what's wrong with it and that's because I'm ignorant when it comes to car engines. So it's OK to be ignorant in some areas of your life.

What's not OK is being ignorant in the areas that are calling you. You just can't be who you really are without being able to hear, understand and converse with the sweet things that are calling you. You do that through understanding. Firstly by understanding yourself, and then understanding how best to put yourself to work so you can get in harmony with what's calling you.

It's only you who can do it. Not your spouse. Not your kids. Not your colleagues. Not your neighbours. This is personal development. It's personal. Only you can do it. So you need to know who you are.

Bill Gove, often dubbed "the father of professional speaking", is the man who paved the way for the speech workshops you see today. He said it best when Bob Proctor heard him say to a live audience at one of his talks, "If I want to be free, I've got to be me. Not the me you think I should be, not the me I think my wife thinks I should be, not the me I think my kids think I should be. If I want to be free, I've got to be me, so I better know who me is."[6]

That strikes a chord with me because I watch most people dive head first into personal development seeking freedom. Financial freedom. Freedom from negative thoughts. Freedom from fat. Freedom from pain. But freedom is a personal thing and what freedom means is different for every person.

So the question is, how can you be free when you don't even know yourself?

The brutal answer is that you can't. But when you understand that there's no limit to what your marvellous mind can achieve, you'll start to rekindle the flame of faith that burned so brightly when you were a child. You'll reunite with all of the dreams you cast aside by settling for what all the people around you still refer to as "the real world". As you

---

[6] Proctor, B. (2018) *Who are you pretending to be? - Proctor Gallagher.* https://www.proctorgallagherinstitute.com/13079/who-are-you-pretending-to-be.

tune back in with yourself, you'll raise your level of consciousness to the altitude of greatness.

You'll know in your heart of hearts that the only problem you're ever going to have in life is you. That the only person who can hold you down is you. That no one else can make you feel inferior without your consent. That you are the captain of your ship. You set the sail.

## Tap into the power of change

To nod your head in agreement is one thing. To fully internalise it all takes a fair amount of understanding of who you are, what you are and how you work. Without knowing these things, you don't know what you're up against. You don't know how to overcome the natural resistance you feel to change. You won't know you'll be fighting an unseen enemy when you try to change. After a while, this causes you to think false, downbeat and unhelpful things like, "That's just the way I am," and that's when the doubt creeps in.

A leopard can't change its spots because it's a leopard. But that's where you and I are different. We can change our spots, behaviours and beliefs because we possess an awesome power to change. It's what separates us from the entire animal kingdom.

Your creative faculties are your invisible powers that give you the ability to change yourself and your environment. You've been given the privilege of choice, the superpower to accept or reject the thoughts, ideas and suggestions that are flowing to you.

## Understanding the conscious and subconscious mind

In turn, you have the mental resources to form any picture you want to see in your mind. Through your feelings, you can fall in love with your own thoughts, ideas and suggestions that cause images or pictures to flash up in your mind. That means you can escape from your present situation any time you like and plunge your consciousness into the state of your wish already being fulfilled. The beauty of doing this is that your subconscious mind is always acting on the suggestions you give it. It doesn't take breaks, talk back or sit around stroking its chin wondering whether the suggestions are in real life or not.

The subconscious mind is a manifester of the thoughts, ideas and suggestions that are continually impressed on it through conscious thought. When you take a high-level look at the mind, you'll see your mind is divided in half and has two spheres of activity: the conscious and the subconscious. It doesn't take much to get these working in unison for you so you can start living the life you truly want to live, but it all starts with pictures.

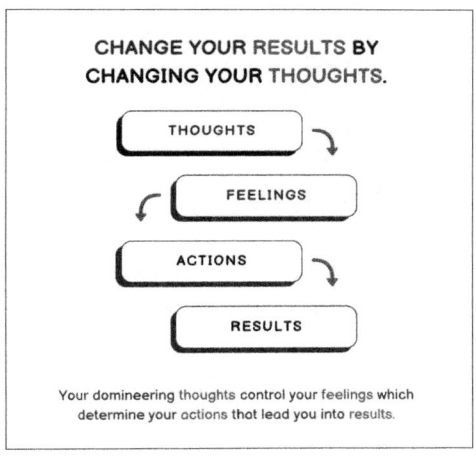

So the question is, what picture pops into your mind when you think of your mind? If you're like most people, you'll visualise a picture of the brain – this kind of purple thing that looks like a slab of congealed gloop that wobbles, or that's often referred to as looking like a walnut or an intestine. This picture comes from being shown what a brain looks like when we were at school, but this picture of the brain doesn't explain the mind any more than a fingernail does.

Now, if you don't have a picture of your own mind, there's no way you can have any idea of how it works, let alone know how to use it for your benefit. There are two levels of your mind, let me explain how these work.

The conscious part of your mind is your "thinking mind". It has the ability to accept or reject the thoughts, ideas and suggestions that are flowing to it from both the outside and the inside world. It works both inductively and deductively. If you don't take up the role of minding the door of your conscious mind, it remains in a deductive state and will accept whatever's thrown at it. That's a bad strategy for those of us who are not where we want to be because we're leaving ourselves wide open to negative influence. With anything and everything allowed to be dumped into our conscious mind, we're impressing a helter-skelter of ideas on to our subconscious mind.

When you finally take up the advice of Jim Rohn, a man many consider to be the best thought leader of his time, and actually "stand guard at the door of your mind"[7], you're actively assessing what's nonsense and what's helpful. You're deciding what suggestions are allowed in and which ones to send on their way. You're controlling the flow. You're wisely filling up your consciousness with positive influence, and you're curating a consistent, congruent ideal that you want to impress upon your subconscious mind.

That's a good thing because the subconscious is what makes you limitless. It's been referred to as many different things over the years, such as infinite intelligence, the higher power, the heart or even God sending you guidance. Make no mistake, you're guiding yourself through your subconscious mind. It's working night and day for you.

The tremendous power of the subconscious mind was summed up perfectly in Napoleon Hill's book, *Think and Grow Rich*, where he shares a quote from one of the richest Americans of his time Andrew

---

[7] Masculinity Highlights (2023) *Stand guard at the door of your mind: Jim Rohn.* https://www.youtube.com/watch?v=ysTE8jhWrdQ.

Carnegie, "Any idea that's held in the mind that's either feared or revered will begin at once to clothe itself into its physical counterpart."[8] This statement has been proven true time and time again. Every man-made material thing in the outside world once only existed in one person's mind. If you ask those people how they came up with the idea, they can't explain it. The best they can do is say they were daydreaming, a thought flashed up in their mind one day and they took action on it.

Take a look around you right now. Maybe you're at home and you see your TV, your canvas picture, your iPhone, your lamp, your air freshener plugged into the wall. Not so long ago, all of these things only existed as a picture in one person's mind.

Due to the creative faculties of your mind, you also have the ability to visualise that which is not already in your physical world. When you think of your house, phone or car, you see pictures of your house, phone or car in your mind. In the same way your mind brings up a picture of what is in your immediate environment, it can just as easily bring up a picture of what's not in your immediate surroundings.

Think of an elephant, a Ferrari, a desert or a beach, and pictures of those things all flash up in your mind. And yet, none or not all of those things are in your immediate environment. The reason you can do this is through using the creative faculty of your mind called perception. Perception gives you the marvellous ability to form pictures in your mind. It's like a magic wand that allows you to see things in your mind that the naked eye cannot see in its vision. It's your very own time machine and movie maker, if you will.

To give you some real-life examples, President Kennedy saw a man walking on the moon in his mind long before the world saw it with their eyes. Steve Jobs saw music in people's pockets in his mind way before he saw the iPod. Liam Gallagher saw himself as a rockstar long before he became one – the one thing all of these people have in common is that

---

[8] Hill, N. (2016) *Think and Grow Rich: The Classic Edition: The All-Time Masterpiece on Unlocking Your Potential--In Its Original 1937 Edition.* Penguin.

they all achieved their visions through the creative faculty of perception.

These people didn't get lucky and stumble upon a good idea. They were:

**Labouring
Under
Correct
Knowledge**

Whether they were aware of it or not.

A major part of why so many people are stuck where they are and they don't know why is that we've become obsessed with developing the intellect and have neglected our ability to think. We've loaded many people up with all these degrees, but to the point they can barely afford their rent. We've preached a promise of if you do well in school, you'll get a good job. If you work hard, you'll earn lots of money. If you earn lots of money, you'll live a good life. None of this is true.

If it were true, there wouldn't be so many school dropouts living mortgage-free in their mansions. There wouldn't be so many people working 60-hour weeks for minimum wage. There wouldn't be so many millionaires who are suicidal…

### The school dropout

A 17-year-old Lord Alan Sugar started out in business by selling reconditioned televisions from his London home in 1965. This led him to start his first business, Amstrad, in 1968 with £100 worth of Post Office savings. He is now, as of 2023, reported to have a personal net worth of £1.21 billion off the back of a stream of successful business

## Chapter 1: You Are Limitless

ventures.[9] He openly admits he's just a simple man from Hackney with no degrees in business and very little schooling, having dropped out of school at 16 years old. Lord Sugar is an example of someone with very little formal education who has achieved the success that they set out to achieve.

### Minimum wage for minimum life

I worked with some fantastic people in the removals industry who are away from home five days a week driving around the UK and Europ`s off. The work is long, physical and very taxing on the body, so when a day off comes, you need that day to recover and don't feel like playing the role of parent or spouse. The last thing on your mind is the thought of popping to the gym to lift some weights or get on the treadmill.

Now, due to the swaying motion of the housing market, the yo-yoing of mortgage interest rates, and the fact that we're all generally happy to blow our entire budget on the purchase of the nicest house we can buy, people who are moving home and require services are somewhat strapped for cash. These are just some of the many factors that put a huge strain on the removals industry. Not to mention the seasonal aspect of the trading year. All in all, the removals industry pays very close to minimum wage because it has to make a profit and keep its workforce employed, but that's not much consolation for those working 60 hours a week in the industry to barely make ends meet.

### The suicidal superstar

Or what about Marshall Mathers? Better known by his rap name Eminem, he burst onto the music scene in 1999 with his Slim Shady

---

[9] Gruffydd, M. (2023) "Alan Sugar is one of UK's 177 billionaires – his huge fortune unveiled," *Express.co.uk*, 20 January. Available at: https://www.express.co.uk/life-style/life/1723549/lord-alan-sugar-net-worth-2023.

LP that he followed up a year later with an album that sold 1.76 million copies in the first week.[10] He achieved his dream of being a rap superstar, and yet in 2007 he survived a near-fatal overdose after becoming dependent on prescription drugs.

## Accessing the limitless you

*Those stories challenge deeply held beliefs that many of us have from childhood – that we need to finish school and get a degree to succeed in business; that if we work hard we'll succeed; that money brings us happiness.* If you're anything like me, almost everything you were raised to believe is not true. The people who raised me weren't bad people who told me lies. They just passed on what was taught to them. They didn't know. They didn't even know that they didn't know.

If you're in the same boat as me, I need you to know that all that you need to succeed is already inside of you. It's just a matter of knowing what you've got going for you and knowing how to draw it out.

You have all of these creative faculties that continue to shape the world at your fingertips. Through the conscious use of your perception, imagination, will, reasoning, memory and intuition, you are limitless.

Even though you are limitless, to be the limitless you is to conform to a new way of life. It all starts with a conscious, committed decision to change. To have an awareness of your boundless power to change and to fall in love with the idea that you could be, do and have the good that you desire.

The reason why it takes a committed decision is because everything in this world has an opposite – good vs bad; rich vs poor; happy vs sad. It's one of the laws of the universe – the Law of Polarity – you can't have one without the other.

---

[10] *Eminem breaks sales record with the Marshall Mathers LP – May 30, 2000* (no date). https://calendar.songfacts.com/may/30/13466.

## Chapter 1: You Are Limitless

Take this book, for example. There's a *front* and a *back* to the book. An *inside* and an *outside*. A *left side* and a *right side*. A *top* and a *bottom*. You can't have one without the other. I find this comforting because if you look for something *wrong* with this book, the only possible reason you'll find it is because there's something *right* with the book. That's how it works.

The challenge that most of us have is that we want one thing without the other. We want to *get* the good that we desire, but not at the expense of *giving up* the things that are blocking us from getting the good that we desire.

That's why the Law of Polarity is an essential law to understand. I've developed the habit of using this law to harvest the crops of good that are present in every situation. Why? To keep me feeling in control and to keep the presence of faith and optimism in my life. Finding the good in negative thoughts, situations and circumstances helps to keep you away from the victim mentality.

My 17-year-old son is a boxer. He came back from the gym one night and was talking about how his right hooks are weak and he always gets hit with uppercuts because his guard is too flimsy and open. This was the story he was telling himself. I advised him to consider the opposite and play a trick on his mind by telling himself that his right hooks were powerful and that his guard was rigid and closed. After telling himself this over and over again in his mind, his right hooks hurt (take it from me) and he comes home from the gym with fewer nosebleeds because his guard blocks far more incoming punches.

To apply this to the concept of becoming limitless, when you make the decision to be the limitless you, you're not only accepting that there's a better way for you to do things, but you're also accepting that what you're doing now is not working, that what you're doing now is wrong. That's a bitter pill to swallow, too bitter for most people. So they spit it out before they even get started. And that's OK – as long as they're happy, I'm happy.

Like a pebble that's dropped into a lake, when you make a committed decision to change, there's always going to be a rippling effect that alters the entire shoreline of your life.

I'm sure you're getting this now, but let me tell you the same thing in a different way to ram my point home and goad you over the line.

To be willing to install new behaviours and new beliefs that line up with the good that you desire is also to be willing to break down old habits and dismantle old beliefs that are in conflict with the good that you desire. Let's face it, who wants to flush out the habits that bring us instant comfort and short-term pleasure?

Even as I write this line I'm thinking that I'd love to be drinking a pint of lager with my friends on this warm summer evening. Instead, I'm sitting in a room on my own, pulling my hair out writing this book. But I'm also thinking that I want to write a book that's going to be, look and feel like one of the jewels of the universe. Sitting in a beer garden right now is not going to move me towards my want to write this book.

It's vital that we listen and tune into our wants, because our wants come from the essence of who we are.

## Make a committed, conscious decision

So, without a committed, conscious decision, there's no way you can stay on track. Before you know it, you'll revert back to doing things the way you've always done them, your results will stay the same and your wants hush into the background noise of the everyday. The bright lights of your brilliance will be dimmed once again.

A committed decision is more than just a hunch, more than just a nice thing to say. It's more like a vow that requires vision, desire and courage.

Sure, as you move through life, you'll develop wisdom and courage. Life experience drip-feeds you enough wisdom and courage to get by, but you're not here just to get by. You are limitless. I believe we're all here to leave the world a better place than we found it.

If you rely on growing your awareness through life experience, by the time you've developed yourself to the point of being attractive to the good that you desire, you could find yourself too old to go after some of the things you wanted in life. Your vision ends up in the rear-view mirror and it becomes something you look back at instead of forward to.

I'm sure you've run into these wise and elderly people yourself. They all say the same things to you, don't they? They tell you to not take life too seriously. To always be grateful. To enjoy life and not waste any time. To go after what you want.

You always feel your heart drop don't you? There's a splash of sadness in their words because you never thought that these wise, courageous people with nerves of steel once felt like you. Afraid. Snookered. Not knowing which way to turn. Fear caused them not to pursue their own dreams when they were in their prime, so they didn't. And now they wish they had because they know life's too short to be afraid. So much so, they cannot bear to see younger people not pursue their dreams.

Imagine reaching a stage of your life when your mind is sharp as a tack and your body is physically unable to gallop towards the ideas you fell in love with? You're seeing the nurse's helpless eyes well up with tears as you tell her the story of how you nearly made it. You're in a hospital bed with your eyes closed watching the movie of your life, and you run into your unfulfilled vision. Don't do it to yourself.

If you've put your plans down, pick them back up right now. Go out there and fail in a glorious fashion if you have to. Fail your way to success if need be.

Make a committed decision that you are prepared to galvanise the magnificence that's waiting within you; that you'll stand up to fear and shake hands with faith; that you'll persist until your potential is realised. Excellence is nothing more than a commitment to completion.

No one wants this written on their gravestone, "Nice person. Could have done more. Never did decide if persistently doing more was ever worth it."

**LIMITLESS SUCCESS HABIT /** Make a decision to change in just one area of your life. It could be something small – like my son developing his right hook – or it might be bigger, like starting your own business. The key to this habit is the commitment that accompanies the decision. Commit to that decision with all of your being and watch the magic happen.

### Tap into the essence of who you are

Remember that your wants come from the essence of who you are, from the biggest part of you that's unseen because it's non-physical. This part of you is always seeking expression. It's the spiritual you living in a physical body who's been blessed with a supercomputer mind that functions through two spheres of activity and is yet to be beaten by logic.

Ideas come into you on a conscious level from other people and you have the ability to accept or reject them. You can *originate* ideas in your mind and you have the ability to accept or reject them. No other life form has this power at their disposal that we're aware of.

The subconscious level is automatic. It has no reasoning factor and can only accept the ideas the conscious level has accepted. Through repetition, feelings and actions, those ideas impregnate the subconscious and are followed by historical moments, like Roger Bannister running a four-minute mile, man walking on the moon or the release of the iPhone, which shock the world.

For you and I, it doesn't have to be that dramatic, but I'm sure you get the gist of the invisible power you have at your disposal.

When you're not aware of your boundless power to change, you won't realise that you're putting the brakes on yourself simply by how you choose your thoughts – by thinking that you can't do something, that you're not that kind of person and (the best one of all) that you don't have enough time.

Time is your most valuable resource. You're limitless, but your time isn't. So much can be done with time. But I get it: you have daily

## Chapter 1: You Are Limitless

obligations, errands and responsibilities to cover before your time is yours. You don't have enough time. You need more time.

If this sounds like you, let me introduce you to a harsh truth that might offend you.

# YOU ARE TIME

Don't let the smiling faces of society fool you. They may meet your "I don't have time" excuse with puppy dog eyes in the moment, but the second your back is turned, those tender-hearted faces transform into images of a hard-faced headmistress with raised eyebrows, and for good reason.

An adult yodelling, "I don't have time" is like a child telling the teacher, "The dog ate my homework." No mature adult truly believes this made-up tale saves them face in the moment. It just doesn't. Let's face it. Everyone knows that the laziest possible excuse for not getting something done is "I didn't have time." You know this too.

People get lied to all the time, and they know when they're being lied to. So, even when you think you've convinced the person you've lied to, you really haven't. They were just polite enough not to call you out on it. You know this better than anyone because the victory you set out to achieve and then accomplished feels very anti-climatic. Not only that, but you feel like you're being confronted by something else. And you are – something you can't manipulate with your sweet talk. Your inside world.

I know I sound harsh because you're rushed off your feet all day, every day. I get it, but the truth is the truth. It can be ruthless and insensitive, which is a good thing, so you always know where you are with it. The truth doesn't tell you what you want to hear. It tells you how it is.

It doesn't care about your feelings, that you have a full-time job, the school run or an elderly relative to care for. Or that you're chasing your tail everyday with your mouth dry, your stomach growling and your head spinning. The truth doesn't sound very nice at all when you think about it, but the truth can set you free. All the chains that bind you to average can be unshackled if you have the courage to confront them.

The truth always means well. It only comes across abruptly when you don't like the truth of the situation you're in. So, use a second for yourself right now, take a deep breath and make a silent pledge to get to the bottom of why you always feel short-changed when it comes to time.

When you're ready to absorb the truth, you're better positioned to cut the crap for good and get to the bottom of your time constraints once and for all.

Ready to absorb a bombshell?

The REAL and ONLY reason why you'd say "I don't have time" is because you've allocated your time to do something else you deem MORE important. Am I right? Of course I'm right.

I know because I'm human and I catch myself saying, "I don't have time" too. When I notice I'm doing it I mentally give myself a slap on the wrist for trying to swerve the truth of the matter. You and I choose what we do with our time. So, it's not about the time, it's about what we choose to do.

### You are time

The study of time has baffled the greatest of minds for thousands of years, but I feel Albert Einstein put it best. He came to the conclusion that you are time.[11] This makes perfect sense to me because when you

---

[11] Hendricks, G. (2009) *The Big Leap: Conquer Your Hidden Fear and Take Life to the Next Level.* Harper Collins.

## Chapter 2: You Are Time

really think about it, time only exists in your consciousness while you exist. If you didn't exist, you would have no concept of time.

I think what Einstein was getting at is that time is an inside awareness rather than an outside measurement. That, even though the time that you and I have is finite, it's much more of an inner countdown than an outer chase, which totally resonates. I mean, it's not like you can catch up to time anyway. God knows, I've tried and I'm sure you have too.

So, the next time you're being heckled by a clock, just remember, without you, there is no time.

You don't need to find, save, or create time. It's already here. Time is omnipresent. It's not into hide and seek. It's in constant supply. Time ticks away in your heart.

I'd like to share a story with you.

It's about a good friend of mine who taught me all I ever needed to know about time in the most unusual form of communication.

As you do, by my mid-thirties I'd lost touch with a fair few of my good friends. This friend I had met through football and then lost touch with was married with children, just like me. He worked 40–50-hour work weeks and had a mortgage, just like me. Both of us were littered with all the usual excuses that come gift-wrapped and packaged in your own little bubbles of boloney.

Anyway, every few months we'd bump into each other amidst the after-school activities, the grocery shop, in the high street and so on. Every time we'd clasp eyes on each other we'd end up acting out the awkward, unconvincing charade of saying, "Let's go out for a beer and watch the football soon," or, "Send me a message and let's meet up for a catch-up." Sound familiar?

We never did meet up. Why? No time.

One day I woke up with this new perspective and thought, "Einstein is right, I am time."

I realised that I held time in my hands like a full hand of cards, and I could play my hours any way I liked. I could move the workday and slide all of life's obligations to one side any time I liked, so that's what I did.

It was a bold move but I was so glad I did. I enjoyed spending the whole afternoon having a few laughs, a bite to eat and a few drinks in my friend's favourite snooker club. The sun was shining, cold drinks were flowing and the responsibilities of life melted into nothingness. This is what living is. I get it now.

Why didn't I do this earlier?

It was a good day. It would have been a great day if it didn't happen to be his wake.

That's right, you heard me. The day of his funeral.

The reason I'm telling you this is because that day I learned that I had always had time in the palm of my hands at all times – that I was time. From that day forward, I knew I'd never again be able to shift the blame of not getting something done or not showing up for someone on time without a conscience.

Consider this: the children of career-minded parents never grow up saying, "Time cared more about work than me when I was growing up. Time didn't give my parents enough time so I had to play ball on my own." That would be inaccurate. Time isn't the villain. What you do, where you are, and who you're with is down to the choices you make. Time has no say in any of it.

I learned another lesson that day: time only exists for you because you exist.

Nothing like a friend's suicide to drop you into the lava of life and make you pop your head up from the clouds of self fabrication. It shouldn't have taken my friend's death to wake me up, to prise my eyes away from my own needs and duties and to burst my own self-centric bubble. How stupid did I feel showing up for him when he couldn't physically show up himself. "Too little, too late" springs to mind.

Of course, I wasn't the only one. Culprits crowded the room. Of course, most of them didn't know it and they probably still don't know it today.

In the midst of life, we risk blinding ourselves with our own dramas and duties so much that we don't notice people dying in front of us. Me and a room full of good-natured, grieving villains were guilty of it. The penny dropped like a lead balloon. In a less extreme circumstance, these people (including me) wouldn't all be off work at the same time meeting up for a social.

### We all have a choice

Getting back to you, I beg you to become acutely aware that you always have a choice. You can be anywhere you choose at any time – within reason, of course. I mean, you can't physically be in New York City and then be in London five minutes after deciding to go there.

What I'm trying to say is that you're nothing like all the other forms of life that are driven to spend their time strictly by their genetic code. But this fact is a double-edged sword. All other forms of life must strive to their maximum potential, but you don't. You can sit, sleep or slouch on the dock of the bay for days and not get eaten by prey. You can scroll through social media all day and night and not go hungry.

You can start as many things as you want and never finish any of them. The tree doesn't have this choice. It must grow as high as it can. You don't. You can leave all kinds of half-baked things dotted around and no one bats an eyelid.

What humans and trees have in common is that they both have their own unique time frame. What they do within their time frame is non-identical. The tree is infatuated with growth and spends every living second seeking out light and reaching up. Trees are laser focused. Humans, on the other hand, are so easily persuaded and distracted by short-term incentives that use up their time and keep them in the shadows – social media, Netflix and Xbox spring to mind. Put it this way, it doesn't take a chainsaw to knock a human off course. What the tree doesn't have to deal with is someone telling them they're not good enough or that they'll never amount to anything.

### Who The Hell Are You?

You might be a thick-skinned, resilient so-and-so who's putting the hours in. I salute you for doing so. The question is, what are you putting into the hours? When it comes to attitude, if you put a whole lot in, you get a whole lot out. When it comes to results, it's what you put in the cake mix that matters the most. The fastest way to halt your passion and wane your enthusiasm is by whisking away for hours without the right ingredients in the bowl.

Take it from me, I am an expert at spinning my wheels. I'm the master of starting things and not finishing them, so I can give you excellent advice here. Through the merit of my desire to do well, my impatience and my lack of direction, I ended up with an impaired vision that dampened my impact on many things. My desire to do well at something, anything, was the underlying pitfall in my quest to do well. I was spending all of my time scatterbrained instead of being laser focused on one thing. My attention beamed all over the place. Startup projects littered the floor.

Having said that, I've also been guilty of staying way too long in a business model that goes against my ideals. A business where the more successful I got, the more free time I lost out on. This made me short with my team and customers. It also left me tired, burnt out and agitated at weekends, which depreciated not only my time, but also the time of the people around me. It wasn't fair on anyone. No one was winning.

All because I didn't know myself well enough. I didn't know that I'm more of a right-brain person who builds up energy and good feeling by feeding off of intuition, daydreams and rhythm. I had no clue I'd anchored myself to a business model that required huge amounts of left-brain functions that stretched my physical senses and left me feeling mentally beaten down, battered and bruised everyday.

I always remember one of my school teachers saying I was a right-brain person because I'm a left-handed writer. I had no clue what she meant, but I often recall her telling me this, even though I'm not even sure being a left-handed writer automatically means you're a right-brain person.

Anyway, the left part of the brain is where the logic lies. You can

Chapter 2: You Are Time

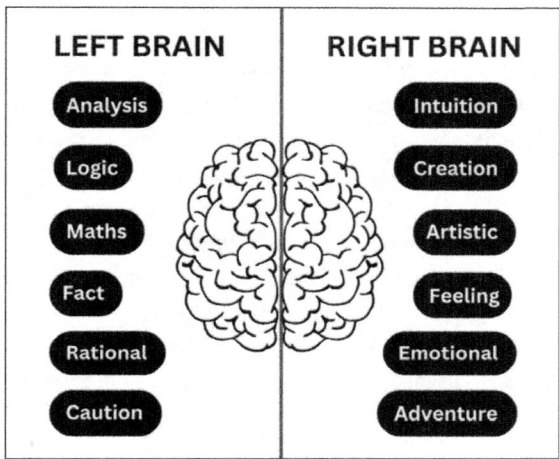

spot left-brain people because they know all the details about the most bizarre things. They remember the facts and they're very analytical. Their ideas are born out of calculations and data. If you're in need of a good accountant or a finance manager, these are the people you want. They'll make sure everything is accounted for and will provide you with accurate forecasts based on past and present data.

The right part of the brain is where creativity is. You'll see these people move with feeling rather than make decisions based on percentages. They're known for being big thinkers and even considered to be living in la-la land at times. They're often artistic and will take roles in design and marketing so they can be intuitive and let their imagination run wild. They're great for building a long-term vision and getting everyone to buy into it. You don't want right-brain people keeping your books though, because they'll really struggle to concentrate on this type of task. If you give them a letter to post, they'll probably forget.

If I had known that part of me was spiritual and the other part physical, I'm sure I would have worked out sooner that the rewards from the business I gave my spirit to derived purely from the physical plane. What I'm trying to say is that right-brain people are best placed in marketing, visionary, writing or design roles because this allows them to create something from nothing that presently exists in the physical world. This work feeds their spirit and keeps them feeling good.

By contrast, left-brain people are best placed in accounting, operations, filling or management roles because they enjoy bringing order to an existing reality. They like to examine and suss out disorder so they can find ways to keep everything tidy, well-presented and performing at a high level. They take the existing tools, spreadsheets and operations manuals and keep everything ticking over as it should on a physical level.

For example, a left-brain person loves a jigsaw, a Rubik's cube, a broken car engine or a wordsearch because they view life through the lens of logic.

A right-brain person loves a blank canvas because they enjoy expressing themselves through creating something from the depths of their own mind.

So there I was, the unfulfilled right-brain business owner pulling his hair out over moving pieces of furniture from one house to another. I was totally unaware that I was bringing order to an existing reality, and that my shoes would have been better filled by a left-brain person.

Had I not done the work to find out who I was, I would still be banging my head against a brick wall running that business now, still thinking I wasn't cut out for business, when the truth was, there was no spiritual nourishment in my business. Simple as that. Therefore, I was not building myself up each day, I was being broken down. With a goal of safely moving more boxes in less time by hand than the previous day, it got monotonous and repetitive. The danger is the comfort that comes with the normal. You work on autopilot, blink and then five years have passed you by with zero progression.

It makes you want to grab time by the scruff of the neck and make it your servant, your antidote to chaos. There's no question about it, time is the most valuable resource you're ever going to have when all is said and done. It's just that when you really think about it, time is not tangible. You are. You can only get a hold of yourself and make the changes by taking the action that moves you towards the good that you desire.

You'll never get time into a headlock until it taps out to your ways, but you can kick yourself into gear. Time can't tap you on the shoulder and give you the nod that "the time is now right" to pursue your wants, but you can have a stern word with yourself.

You've just got to accept that time slips away easier than water runs through your fingertips. Stomping on through jubilation and heartache, it struts past death, divorce or your birthday without so much as a backward glance. It's a loose cannon. You, on the other hand, are manageable. Time can't be changed, but you can. You can double your productivity with a few subtle changes that are relatively painless. The goal is to get more from yourself so that you can accomplish in an hour what used to take a week.

### Divide to multiply

This system was shown to me by a man who buys, builds and sells businesses – Brad Sugars. He's been the CEO of nine-plus companies, has been business coaching since 1993, and grew his one-man business coaching company into a worldwide franchise. Divide to multiply is such a simple and powerful concept, where the idea is to divide up a task and multiply the outcome. First, you must be aware of the tasks that gulp down the most of your time because they require your time, energy and effort. When you've exposed your time-sucking tasks, think: automate, delegate, eliminate.

Let's say you want to get more customers for your retail store. Well, you can't directly get more customers – unless you pull people into your shop against their will, put a gun to their head and force them to buy. But you can get more leads and you can increase the conversion rate of those leads, which results in more customers. A question would be: how can I automate the lead flow of my business to free up some of my time?

You can use the same formula when it comes to making the family breakfast. Divide the end result to multiply the outcome. Get the bowls, spoons, cups and cereal box out of the cupboard the night before so breakfast is swiftly made in the morning.

Choose your clothes for the following day the night before. Take them out of the wardrobe and put them somewhere neatly so you can wake up without having to wrestle with coat hangers or decide what to wear for the day. It's all been decided, prepared and is ready for you to get dressed.

At work, if you find yourself writing out the same email again and again, instead of typing out the same sentences that results in taking two minutes to send the email, set up a prewritten quick step email so you can get the email sent in ten seconds.

The compound effect of dividing up your tasks to multiply the outcome fuels you with confidence, keeps you relaxed and helps you stay on top of everything.

Simply put, we can spend or invest our time. Spend time watching Netflix. Invest time writing this book. Spend time scrolling on social media. Invest time meeting up with friends. I suggest you spend less time watching the clock tick and invest more time working on the things that make you tick.

Orison Swett Marden was an inspirational author who wrote about the principles of success and said in his book *He Who Thinks He Can*, "People do not value the immense power of utilising spare minutes."[12] Again, the "utilising" is a doing word that comes from within and a belief that the progress made by taking action even in small amounts of time will amount to taking big strides towards victory.

---

[12] Marden, O.S. (2017) *He Can Who Thinks He Can, An Iron Will & Pushing to the Front: How to Achieve Self-Reliance Which Leads to Vigorous Self-Faith, Personal Growth & Success..* e-artnow.

### Come back to the here and now

Time ticks away in your heart. It's not the measure of a timepiece that's set to a universal set of digits – that's just the best system available to control people and things that happen in the outside world. The clock is handy for keeping tabs on yourself, other people and when the check-in gate at the airport is closing, but although helpful in some areas, it can be a total hindrance and wreak havoc with our inside worlds.

Every strike of the clock drives a sane person crazy somewhere, whether they're waiting for a bus, a friend or a dentist appointment. Handmade identities are being formed about other people based on their good or bad time keeping skills. Dare not be late if you don't want to be labelled arrogant, disrespectful and uncaring. Dare not be early if you don't want to be stamped as Mr or Mrs Perfect.

When push actually comes to shove and you poke around for some tangibles, the only thing you or I can control is what we do with our time in the here and now. The only thing we truly own is this moment in time.

So the next time your head is mashed and you are feeling frazzled with life, ask yourself two simple questions. Where am I? What time is it?

The only undeniable answer you're ever going to get from those two questions are "here" and "now". Where am I? Here. What time is it? Now. This helps you feel grounded. It gives a little time out from the stretching, closing the gap between your physical and non-physical senses. Sometimes, when the day gets the better of us, our physical and non-physical senses go into overdrive and can act on autopilot without our full consent. When this happens, you'll feel out of control.

### Activate your time machine

Time is a silent assassin that marches on in sync with a gazillion army boots.

And that's OK because your mind is a time machine. You can close your eyes and transport yourself to any place you like at any time you like. You can take yourself to the future, relive the past or contemplate the present whenever you want. You can think of your dream car and put yourself in it no less than a second after closing your eyes. Shutting down the physical sense of sight in exchange for the higher faculty of perception is a daily habit every conscious, competent person swears by. They imagine and sharpen up the details of their better future by using their mind, taking themselves out of the madness of today so they can focus on the saneness of tomorrow.

I suggest you start using your creative faculties to clearly design your future and start feeding your mind with the good that you desire. This will activate your reticular activating system (RAS). Your RAS makes you notice specific things. To give you an example of how this works, imagine you want a new car in a specific model and colour, because there aren't many around. Once you connect to that want, suddenly you start seeing the car everywhere you go. Here's the thing: the cars were always there, your brain was just not trained to look for them before. That's how the RAS in your mind works. To use this to your advantage, you need to get really clear on what you want in the future.

Hope in the future gives you power in the present. All of us can grow in ways we've not even thought of yet. You can add mega value to the world in ways you've not yet imagined. It's OK to think about the future when your eyes are closed. By doing so, you'll have raised your awareness in the present when your eyes are open.

It's all too easy to not consciously remove our steamed-up goggles of the day, and let our days morph into one through neglect until an entire lifetime has washed by. The word on the street is that your whole life flashes before your eyes before you die. Is that why you see old people gathered in the lounges of care homes all asleep? Are they really asleep in that armchair or are they watching the movie of their life? Reflecting, reframing and picking out the best advice possible so they can warn the future generation of the pitfalls of life, even though they know the younger generation are just going to smile back at them in pity. They still try anyway.

The latter years of your life are the perfect time to analyse your life – how well you, as the lead character, performed. How many people feel like an extra in their own movie, I wonder? Perhaps those who gave up on their dreams and spent the last months of their lives sitting in armchairs with a blanket, slippers and plenty of shut-eye wondering why.

**TIME SUCCESS HABIT/** To avoid looking back on your life and feeling as though you've only been an extra in your own movie, you have to use your time consciously. Each time you are deciding how to spend your time, take just ten seconds to ask yourself, "Why this activity?" and follow that up with, "How will this bring me closer to my version of success?" Be honest with your answers. You might discover you spend a lot of your time on activities that hold you back – don't beat yourself up, because now you know this you can make conscious decisions to spend your time on activities that move you forward and help you grow.

### Check your attitude

What's your attitude like? A bad attitude in the present stunts growth in the future.

Let's go out on a limb and say it's going to take you ten years to succeed in the area you want to succeed in. That's far too long, right? Well, that time is going to pass anyway. The question is, where will you be? And if ten years is too slow for you to live your dreams, is it faster than never? You have one thing to do. Decide.

I can't get your time. You can't get mine. Even though sharing moments together can feel like the only way we can share time, the truth is that all we're really sharing is perception. If we both turn away from each other, we're no longer sharing time.

No one can give you the time that's yours anyway, but they can take it. And guess what, they will take it if you let them. So be stingy with your time if you have to. It doesn't pay to give too much of your time away to the wrong person. If the time you're giving to a well-paid job isn't being well received by your inside world, you may want to evaluate how many of your 4,000 weeks of life you're willing to part with because of it.

We tell ourselves we haven't got time, but we are time.

Remember that saying, "I just don't have the time," means you're using up your time doing other things you deem MORE important.

You can't save time; you can only save yourself from the madness of the day by getting organised. By setting yourself up for success in advance, you'll wake up with a stack of ammo ready to blast down the entire dilemma of the day before you even leave the house. Prior planning prevents poor performance. It also gives you the superpower to brush aside all the little niggles, hitches and issues and swat the bigger things down like flies.

Most people are coasting along on the road of least resistance. The danger of a comfort zone is that it doesn't hurt and it might even feel good. You'll only remain disgruntled in a comfort zone for reasons relating to doubt and worry.

You heard me; fear is contributing to your wild allegation against time. Many of the choices you make on a daily basis are causing you to spend a great deal of time doing the things you don't want to do, but that you deem more important than doing something else.

I can't get your time, unless you give it to me. Just like no one can get your time, unless you give it to them.

If you deem it more important to give 40 hours a week away to a well-paid job that drains the life out of you over doing something you want to do, you're doing it because you fear losing your well-paid job.

It's less scary to lose your fun than your income. It's less damaging to the outside world too. Losing your income dents your pride and puts a chink in your self-image.

Time will ultimately get the better of all of us, but that doesn't mean you can't glow in the time you have, that you can't rugby tackle your way through the chaos that comes your way.

You can come out on top.

To quickly recap…

## Chapter 2: You Are Time

The human mind has not found a way to squeeze an extra hour out of a 24-hour day, so you have to get a grip of yourself and become more productive with the hours you've got.

No one masters time. You can only manage activities.

The biggest waste of time is spending time attending a time management course on the grounds that time itself can't be managed. Trying to manage time is like standing on the beach trying to hold back the waves. You cannot manage time. You cannot control how fast the clock ticks.

You can only manage and control yourself, and the activities you do that use up your time. You either spend or invest time by what you're doing. It all comes down to what you do with the time you have. It can even impact how good or bad a time other people are having as a result of you. It's always you. Who else could it possibly be? By the choices you make and what you say yes or no to.

So get to it and make the mistakes no one has made before. Or risk living the same life as the unfulfilled people around you who also settled for someone else's lot in life. You weren't born with a perfect spiritual DNA to be a cardboard cut-out of someone who believes more in you than you currently believe in yourself.

You are time. Park your excuses, get yourself in tip-top shape and get more done in a day than the average person does in a month. No one else can bring your A game to the party. Only you can boogie your way through the craziness of the day and leave a legacy within your 4,000 weeks.

Sounds like a lot of work, right? You're out of breath just thinking about it. Your enthusiasm is deflating like a balloon. Well, have I got good news for you.

# YOU ARE ELECTRIC

If you want to know the secrets of the universe, think in terms of energy, frequency and vibration.

**Nikola Tesla**

As a pioneering electrical engineer, Tesla knew plenty about electricity and how it impacts our lives, and he's right – energy, frequency and vibration are the keys to the secrets of the universe, or at least the secrets of your universe. Let me explain.

In the same way that electricity vibrates, so do you. In the same way that electricity emits a pulse, so do you. In the same way that a power lead has an invisible magnetic energy field around it, so do you, which is proved through Kirlian photography, which I'll talk about more later in this chapter. That's what makes you electric. Not only electric, but also a magnet.

That's right, you're a magnet. You're pulling things to you all the time. All of the things that you're vibrating in harmony with. Now, you may not like what you're surrounded by right now, but that's irrelevant; you're vibrating in harmony with it and that's why you have it in your life. Damn it. Another truth bomb.

Now, since the pulse of electric energy is always accompanied by a pulse of magnetic energy, this is another way to say, "The Law of Vibration is always accompanied by the Law of Attraction," which means, in the same way that two power leads vibrating at the same frequency are pulled together by the invisible magnetic field, you too can pull the good that you desire towards you once you're vibrating at the same frequency as it.

This is why so many people lose faith in the Law of Attraction. They don't realise it's a secondary law; that it's a companion of a primary law. Yes, the Law of Attraction is the shop window of the personal development world, but it's still a secondary law. If a man works only on his abs, biceps and chest in the gym, he may beach out his body, but he's not going to get what he wants if that's to win the squat competition.

The Law of Attraction is a razzle-dazzle law of the universe that confuses a lot of people. Goals get written down and closed away in notebooks, dream boards get made and filed away out of sight, out of mind and into digital folders, and all trust is thrust into paper-thin faith for the universe to make it all happen. When it doesn't happen, hope disintegrates. It's no wonder people start thinking it's all a load of codswallop.

Here's the thing to know: all secondary laws remain dormant to your wants until primary laws arouse them. The Law of Vibration is the primary law that rouses the Law of Attraction to your wants. Don't get me wrong, you're always in a vibration, so the Law of Attraction is always working. It just won't be working on what you want unless you're vibrating in harmony with what you want.

Like I've already touched upon, everything you want is already here. It's just vibrating on a different frequency than you. So the goal is to raise your vibration to get yourself on to the same channel as the good that you desire.

If you've never heard of this before, it takes a fair amount of bandwidth to wrap your head around it. So go easy on yourself if this sounds alien to you. None of us are taught to study ourselves and that's why we all risk going through life not knowing an awful lot about ourselves. Stick with me on this. I've got your back.

In short, you're a mass of energy that's vibrating in a physical body, and you're surrounded by an outside world where everything moves and nothing rests, so the whirlwind of energy in the outside world flows to you all of the time. Energy is literally crashing into you. You've been plunked in the same stratosphere as this tornado of energy, so there's no way you can stop it flowing to you. Now, not only does outside energy flow to you, it also flows through you. There's no choice in the matter.

The choice you do have, however, is what type of energy you allow to flow to and through you. For instance, a simple change of environment pipes you up to a whole new flow of energy. Of course, the goal here is to be pummelled with the right energy; the kind of energy that amps you up and supports the way you want to live and how you want to feel. You don't want to be plugged into energy that zaps the zest out of you.

I'm sure you've been around people who bring you down just by being in their presence. It's not that they've done anything to you, and you can't put your finger on why they make you feel that way, or why you just don't click. The answer is energy. Their low state of vibration puts you in a low state of vibration. This is a prime example of putting yourself in an environment where someone else's negative energy flows to you, and you allow it to flow through you. You may think, "I don't feel good," which means you're in a low-energy state. You'll never hear someone say, "I'm consciously aware that I'm in a negative vibration," but you will hear them say, "I don't feel good." When you think this, it's your cue to examine your energetic environment.

Aside from the energy that's outside of you, you can also draw from the infinite supply of energy that's inside of you. This is your inner thought energy that flows into your consciousness and has the power to change your state of vibration for better or worse based on whether you're thinking positively or negatively. This happens when you spend time with your spiritual self and your inner energy, which is the most purified energy you'll ever have the chance to pipe yourself up to. That's why people feel so good after meditating. When you open the floodgates to your inner guidance, you allow the energy to flow through you, which feels liberating, inspiring and free.

So, why does meditation work? When you meditate or even just lie or sit somewhere quietly with your eyes closed, you'll find that the chaos in your head simmers down and your whole body just relaxes on its own. With each breath, your thoughts from the day will clear, your body will calm and that's when you'll notice fleeting thoughts that prod you as if they're trying to tell you something. These thoughts are usually unrelated to the day because these thoughts are ideas that are coming from within. From you. From the non-physical side of you that will never be seen.

Some people call this their space god, spirit, higher self, or even attribute it to their dead relatives. I call it my inner thought universe. Everyone has an inner thought universe and everyone can access it. The ideas that come from your inner thought universe are pure and not influenced by the trivia of the day. They should be encouraged to flow into your consciousness because I believe the answers that you seek are here. Inside.

## Energy flows from high to low

I never used to think too much about the fact that getting out of bed during the week was way harder than the weekend. I'd always need an alarm clock to wake me during the week, and even then I'd hit the snooze button for another 15 minutes. Yet, on the weekend I'd spring out of bed without any form of prompt or self negotiation. This went on for years without me giving it much thought.

So, why did I spring out of bed on the days when I didn't have to get up for work? And on the days I had to work, why did I feel that I was too tired to get up?

Well, it all comes back down to electronics. Ask any electrician and they will tell you that electricity flows from positive to negative. World energy even flows from North to South. Given these facts, and given the idea that you are electric, it's accurate to say that your energy flows from a higher to lower potential too. Why would it not?

When I learned this I suddenly realised why I had energy to do some things and not others. I'd be pumped up to play football because I was thinking positively about it and downbeat when a dinner date loomed with people who I didn't particularly want to be around because I was thinking negatively.

There's an active example of how energy flows from positive to negative in every football dressing room. One player is excited for the game and another is nervous. I know this because I've been both the excited player and the nervous player over the course of my playing days.

Let me tell you, I experience an abundance of energy from the feeling of excitement. When I was locked into a negative polarity and experienced nerves, my energy was out of sync. It expressed itself like a petrol lawnmower with a crinkled fuel pipe. It felt like a battle and I'd often feel like I couldn't get myself out of first gear.

The excitement comes from thinking positively about what's going to go right in the match before it starts. I think about that magical pass I'm going to make and that spectacular goal I'm going to score and on it goes so that every positive thought impulse gets me more and more amped up for the game. If you were to ask me how I'm feeling about the game, I would say something like, "I'm buzzing and can't wait for this match to start."

The nerves came from thinking negatively and focusing on all the things that could go wrong in the match. I used to worry about missing a chance to score a goal and making the wrong pass and on it used to go. Every negative thought impulse would tie my stomach and energy up in knots. If you were to ask me how I was feeling about the game, I would say something like, "I'm nervous and can't wait for this game to finish."

In truth, the feeling is about the same; it was my thoughts that made the energy either flow or crash. Thinking negatively while engaged in action is like swimming against the tide. Whereas thinking positively while engaged in action is such a free flow that it turns into acceleration.

I stay motivated, happy and full of life by keeping myself plugged into the positive potential of life by visualising, designing my future and practising gratitude. Other things I do to stay positive are listening to upbeat music, watching comedy, eating well, exercising, smiling, laughing, joking, studying, speaking in a positive language and being around positive people.

When I'm not being intentional with positivity, the pummelling of the inevitable negative energy that's flowing to me from the outside world sends shockwaves of groggy energy through me, and I end up demotivated.

### Mental alchemy: turning your thoughts into energy

I've no doubt you experience days of feeling like you need to get more energy, but here's the thing: you don't get energy, you release it through desire. The times I've blamed being an introvert as the reason I felt drained when meeting new people is criminal. The truth is, I felt drained because I didn't have the desire to meet new people. I'd thought myself into a bad vibration before I'd even laid eyes on someone, let alone started to shake hands with them.

Just think, when you're feeling sluggish, run down and groggy, the odds are you're not tired at all, you're just in a bad vibration. You can be in a bad vibration by simply being consciously involved with a destructive concept, which is a shame because intelligent action cannot come from a bad vibration. In fact, nothing good comes from a bad vibration. If you find you're mostly in a bad vibration, there's a good chance that you don't have something you're shooting for. That's why goals are so important. Goals build desire, and goals originate from thought.

What's great about that is that our thoughts control our feelings, and then our feelings control our actions which lead to our results.

## Chapter 3: You Are Electric

Your feelings are conscious awareness of your state of vibration. When you feel good and everything falls into place, you're in a positive vibration. When you feel bad and everything you touch breaks, you're in a negative vibration. The way you feel at any particular moment is down to the chemical makeup within your body, but it all starts with thought.

Every thought you have is just a wave of energy that you have the ability to accept or reject. Accepted thoughts spike the rhythm of your body with the same frequency as the accepted thought. Thoughts can build or destroy. They can cheer you up or make you sad. But they have no power until you give them power.

On the face of it, thoughts are nothing more than formless suggestions that drift in and out of your consciousness. They often bear no resemblance to the truth or reality. They show up without form, without meaning and without a pulse. It's only when we give them meaning that they take on a life of their own. They always have, always will and it all seems innocent, but they are the cause of our vibration and the reason for the results we're getting.

Very simply put, negative thoughts put you in a negative state of vibration and leave you feeling agitated or frustrated. On the flip side, positive thoughts put you in a positive state of vibration that makes you feel cool, calm and calculated.

To change the way you're feeling, your outlook and the entire chemical makeup of your body, all you have to do is **think** differently. You hold all of the power. The invisible power of positive change.

Simple, right? Yes. But it's not always easy.

Before we go any further, I'm aware that positive thinking is probably not a revelation to you. You have probably heard about it a hundred times before. And if you're like most people, you tried positive thinking, it didn't work, and you lost faith in the idea.

Let's see if Andrew Carnegie, the great steel merchant, can restore your faith in positive thinking. He said, "Any idea that's *held* in the mind, that is either feared or revered will begin to clothe itself in the most convenient and appropriate forms available."[13]

When you make deliberate use of your creative faculties, you plant the right thoughts in your mind, water them daily, and give them enough time to take root in your mind and move into physical form.

**EXERCISE: HOW TO PLANT THE RIGHT THOUGHTS IN YOUR MIND/** Take 15 minutes of your time today to go someplace where you won't be disturbed and really think about what you want. Close your eyes and allow the thoughts to come into your mind. The thoughts will always come because you're drawing on an infinite source of thoughts, even if you don't realise it.

What you want doesn't have to be a material item like a car or a boat or a house. One thing you could want is to be calm and present on your wedding day. Or to be confident talking in front of large groups of people. Your want belongs to you at the end of the day. It doesn't have to be in fashion or follow the latest TikTok trend.

You'll notice that every thought attaches a picture to itself – whether you think of a house, a boat or about yourself acting in a certain way, you will get a new image each time a new thought flickers through your mind. Once you've got your image, hold it in your mind. Stay with it, zoom in, zoom out, see if you can notice any more details in the image.

Once your 15 minutes are up, transfer the details on to paper by writing a description of your image or even drawing the image. Know that every time you close your eyes, you can return to this place in your mind.

The image is right because it came from you. If you focus on why, you can make that image become your reality, because you'll start attracting a train of thought that helps you get there. These are the right thoughts. You can formulate a plan and start taking the certain action required.

---

[13] *Andrew Carnegie Quote: "Any idea that is held in the mind that is either feared or revered will, begin at once to clothe itself in the most conv..."* (no date). https://quotefancy.com/quote/1122515/Andrew-Carnegie-Any-idea-that-is-held-in-the-mind-that-is-either-feared-or-revered-will.

Do this 15-minute practice tomorrow, and the next day, and the day after, and every day until it becomes hard not to do it. The idea is to flood your mind with what you want.

## Find the right vibration

Because what we think about controls how we feel and sets up our vibration, our vibration is in control of our output and our results. Therefore, if we want to make changes, our vibration needs to be altered.

The goal is simple: to vibrate in harmony with the good you desire as your default state. All of us have experienced short bouts of vibrating in harmony with the good we desire, and have seen short-term results because of it.

We've all watched a motivational video that made us jump off the sofa and inspired us to take massive action in the moment. Then a couple of days later we feel a shadow of the new reformed go-getting us and we go back to being the person we think we are. But that's not true… we've just fallen back into the same vibration as before.

As you're now aware, you and I think in pictures and energy is always flowing to and through us. So it's up to us to control the flow of energy so we can stay in a positive vibration and remain attractive to the good we desire.

When you accept that the energy that's flowing to you is exciting and inspiring, harmonious pictures flash in your consciousness which causes the energy to flow down to the body and motivates you to take the actions you know will make a difference. You do it because of the vibration you're in.

Using the example of the motivational video, here's what happens – you get emotionally involved in a motivational video, ideal **pictures** flash in your mind that stir up a **desire** that sends a surge of **energy** through your body which is expressed there and then. You spring up into steadfast action and start making progress towards the good that you desire.

The only reason your energy in this new area wanes after a few days is because everyday life returns and you lose sight of the picture. You tune back into what's going on around you and your consciousness is plugged back into the same source of energy that's been flowing to you for years.

This is how we keep on falling back to what we **think** is our default state.

We let familiar *pictures* flash in our minds that stir up zero *desire* and that sends lacklustre *energy* through our body, and there you have it. Bam. We're back in the same vibration that we've been in for years getting the same results we've been getting for years. You could almost say it's like taking the red pill to wake up from the Matrix, only to take the blue pill just a day or two later and fall back into the comfortable, but uninspiring, existence you have found yourself in.

See, the inspirational pictures that flashed in your conscious mind and gave you hope faded when you let them – you didn't hold them in your consciousness long enough for your subconscious mind to accept them. As a result, your positive vibration dilutes, you stop taking the new action that gets results, and you're back where you started.

When you're not aware of the higher creative faculties of your mind such as imagination, will, perception, reason, memory and intuition you won't hold your new thoughts in your consciousness with sure-fire intent because you have no reason to. You won't see the point of doing so. You end up believing you're just the way you are: you're bound to be mediocre and you feel trapped there.

You'll resort to your usual reasons for not doing as well as you could. "I just can't do that," "That's not me," "I tried that, but it didn't work." This is not the case. You've just allowed yourself to fall back into your habitual vibration without consciously knowing that's what you've done.

## Become your true magnetic self

The fact remains that the moment you think differently, the chemicals

## Chapter 3: You Are Electric

within your body are different and this changes your emission, your frequency and the pulse you emit. The stronger the pulse, the better you feel, and the more magnetic you are to the good that you desire.

Just as surely as you have the ability to be a magnet to the things you desire, you also have the ability to be a magnet to the things you don't desire. This is why you must study the Law of Vibration if you want to make positive changes.

You don't need to learn how to be a magnet because you are one. You just need to learn how to set the pulse. In other words, how to influence the energy that's flowing into your consciousness so that you can attract your innermost desires. Because, as we've touched upon, the pulse you currently emit is in direct proportion to what's being attracted to you.

You may feel defensive about your current results and that's understandable because you're doing your best. You may know you're boxed in but you don't know why. You may even want to reel off your list of reasons for not doing well up until this point, but the fact is that where you are today is where your thoughts have brought you.

Life throws all kinds of things at us every day to keep our minds busy and our lives full. If we just let the daily trivia run riot and control our thoughts, we'll find ourselves not where we want to be and surrounded by all of these things we don't want.

Everything is coming to all of us in the exact proportion of our vibration.

You see, in one form or another, the good you desire is already here. It's just vibrating on a different frequency than the one you're on. Your present results are not a reflection of who you are. They're nothing more than a manifestation of your thoughts up until this point.

Since we're all subject to laws that are exact, and our success is dependent on how well we bring ourselves into harmony with these laws, what thoughts put you in harmony with the good you desire? If you were to run a movie through your mind, what would the good you desire look like? How would you be dressed? How would you talk? What would the picture look like?

Thought is the most potent energy there is. So much so that where you are today is where your thoughts have brought you. Every thought you have changes your state of vibration, and your state of vibration hooks you up to a frequency where you can only attract what's on the same frequency. In the same way the only difference between water, steam and ice is the state of its vibration. The only difference between you with your ideal life and you without your ideal life is the state of your vibration.

The question is, do you *hate* what you don't desire MORE than you *love* the good you do desire? If you seek the bare-bones truth of what you're in harmony with right now as you read this sentence, the above question requires a fearless and thorough self-examination to get the honest answer to the question. You may not like the answer you find; it may even come as a shock to you and make you second-guess yourself. That's OK. You're starting to take ownership of your life and you're on the way to your version of success by analysing your state of vibration. Only the *truth* will set you free.

In that case, perhaps the most important questions you're ever going to ask yourself are these:

1 Do you hate poverty more than your love for prosperity?
2 Do you hate disease more than you love health?
3 Do you hate work more than you love freedom?

Ever noticed that if you hate something more than you love its opposite, you end up with what you hate? It's simple, if you're giving all of your thought to what you don't want, you're only going to get more of it. If you love it more, it's yours. If you hate it more, it's yours.

Whatever you feel most strongly about is what you have today. That's maybe not what you want to hear but you're subject to universal laws that are exact.

In this case, your thoughts control your feelings, and your feelings control your actions. So if you want to start living life on your terms, you need to get a handle on this, and you have to start at the root cause: your thoughts. If you're giving all of your thought to what you don't want, your attention is beaming energy its way so you're only going to get more of it.

It's like when you give too much thought to an empty bank balance, you start feeling down and act in a way that brings an emptier bank balance your way. When you think you can't win in business, you feel deflated and act in a way that makes you not win at business. If you think you're an unfit person, you'll feel tired and you'll skip the gym.

Notice I say what *you* think, not what other people think. The reason I bring this up is because what other people think or say about you is not important. What you think and say about yourself is everything.

So, remember that what you think about gives you feelings that cause you to act in relation to what you think about. The advice here is to start choosing to think the kind of thoughts that make you feel good and motivate you to take the action that causes good thoughts.

Remember what the famous martial artist and movie star Bruce Lee told the world, "The body always follows the mind."[14]

So, it's one thing saying something. It's something entirely different to do something.

If you feel you're just a negative thinker, stop thinking you are. Read that again.

**ELECTRIC SUCCESS HABIT/** The way you take control of your thinking is through practice. Make a decision that you're going to look for the good in everything. Before you know it, your default setting will be that of a cheery person with a good attitude who's permanently piped up to the frequency of success. This won't happen overnight, but if you seek out the good in every situation, no matter how well hidden it may seem, you will spend more and more time vibrating on the frequency of success.

---

[14] Bruce Lee Quote (no date). https://www.azquotes.com/quote/757203.

The basic point is that the good you desire is singing a different song to you. To get in tune with it, you have to change your thoughts, set up new habits and follow through on your commitment. Basically you have to prime yourself to work in harmony with the Law of Vibration.

Once you're clear on what you want, you just need to raise your vibration to the same level of energy as what you want, and the things you want will be attracted to you.

You have all the knowledge you'll ever need to know already inside of you. It's just a case of drawing it out. You are unique. You mustn't follow the crowd. You must be different – not for the sake of being different, but because you are different. You can hook up to an infinite number of frequencies whenever you want.

Take your mind back to a day in your life when everything just fell into place. What do you remember? By the way, the first picture that flashes in your mind is the correct moment.

How did you *feel* that day when everything just fell into place? Good, right? Everything you touched turned to good. It was as if you could do no wrong. You were on fire. And you probably just put it down to "one of those good days" when everything just worked out.

The truth is, you were in a positive vibration so everything fell right into place.

During that day, life probably felt so effortless – and that's because it is when you're working with the universal laws.

Living a happy, healthy and wealthy life isn't done by accident. There's no coincidence. The laws of the universe are exact. It's purely electronics we're dealing with here – nothing more.

### You're in control

You don't get what you want. You get what you feel.

You can control what's going on inside by blocking out what's going on outside. Nothing else can do that.

## Chapter 3: You Are Electric

When an acorn is buried beneath the ground, energy is instantly attracted to it. Vibrations pick up its movement, harmonise with it and start driving roots down into the ground. Before long, that energy bursts through the earth and shoots up to grow as much as it can.

Here's the thing: an acorn can ONLY grow into an oak tree. A grass seed can ONLY grow into grass. A sunflower seed can ONLY grow into a sunflower.

That's where you're different. You can grow into anything you want because you have the ability to think and vibrate on different frequencies. You can sow any idea in your mind and through tending to it regularly, see the result in its physical counterpart.

You can THINK yourself into the house you want to live in. Think yourself into the car you want to drive. Think yourself into the dream job or the perfect relationship.

But the acorn, the grass and sunflower seed have no choice about what they're going to grow into.

To prove energy is everywhere and it's flowing to and through you all the time, listen to this. If someone's staring at you from across the street, you will feel them staring at you. They're projecting a laser beam of energy into you, and sure enough, you turn around and catch them staring at you.

Energy is flowing to us from the outside world and we have the choice to accept or reject it with our conscious mind. If we accept the energy on a conscious level and get emotionally involved with it, the energy ends up in our subconscious mind, moves down to the body and is expressed in the form of a result.

So it is VITAL that we control the flow of energy that's flowing to and through us at all times so we remain in a good vibration.

That's why they say you're the average of the five people you spend the most time with. It's because their energy is flowing to you and when you spend a lot of time with someone, you connect with them on an emotional level, internalise their energy and you end up in a similar, if not the same, vibration.

See, I was raised to believe that all I had to do was work hard and everything I wanted would all come to me. What I learned was that "hard work" is simply NOT one of the natural laws of the universe, and whenever you're not working with these natural laws, you're going to feel a struggle.

## Change your perception to change your tune

Have you ever been told by someone else to change the record?

I know I have. How rude and disrespectful, right? I've been shocked by it on more than one occasion because I thought that I was talking sense and sharing value. I never realised that I was being too full on and rubbing the other person up the wrong way.

In reality, people don't tell you to change the record because they wholeheartedly disagree with you. It's more of a case of them being unable to understand you by not being tuned into the same frequency as you. They're unable to connect with your ideas because you're on a different wavelength to them.

It's like telling an accountant that marketing is an investment. Most of them will not have it! Trust me. They'll tell you that marketing is an expense.

And the reason why opinion differs is because of frequency. Accountants are dialled into the profit & loss Sheet. Entrepreneurs are dialled into the cash flow report. Both arguments are right because both parties are thinking on different thought waves that beam different perspectives and lead to different forms of success.

Let's say you show the accountant your marketing sheet that shows you're paying £10 out in one marketing strategy that gets you £20 back. Over time you scaled that up to £100 out to get £200 back. It would become obvious to anyone that to get £200 for every £100 that goes out would make that a sound investment.

Now the accountant has changed their perception, they will likely change their tune. With a new-found perspective on the things that limit you, you can also change your tune.

### Break free of the beliefs that hold you back

I was raised in a hard-working family, so they didn't know. So much so, they didn't even know they didn't know. They were great people who were ignorant to the laws of the universe, and therefore violated them without realising and ended up with lesser results than they deserved because they violated the laws.

Mantras like, "You have to work hard for money," are not uncommon. They're often passed down from family generation to generation and on and on it goes. A century passes by and the living members of the family are still vibrating on the same frequency as 100 years before, and they get the same or very similar results to the family members of 100 years before.

It doesn't matter whether we're talking today or a 100 years ago, the human body is as electric today as it ever was in the past or is ever going to be in the future.

I just wish I'd known before spilling bucket loads of blood, sweat and tears that hard work, plans, passion and persistence can only get a driven person so far. When I realised that "hard work" alone just won't do it, it was confusing to me.

I had to unlearn some stuff. I had to get out of the habit of moving furniture and boxes from house to house each day and look inwards instead. I had to go against everything I was raised to believe and had become accustomed to, even though it seemed skewed.

The people who were telling me odd things like, "You need to slow down to speed up," were the same people who were getting the results that I wanted to get. Their way was working and mine was not. So I took a leap of faith. I ran with it and never looked back.

It pains me to see so many people out there right now tearing themselves apart just to end up with the same results this year as they had last year, and the year before that, and the year before that. So many people end up feeling deflated by living a photocopy year for so long that they tend to lose faith that a better year is possible for them, which is just criminal because it's like they're quitting three feet away from the gold. It's criminal because they have got the "work" part sussed.

If I sound like I'm contradicting myself here, please let me explain.

While working with the Law of Vibration is not hard work as you know it, you cannot "Ohm" your way to success. Just like hard work, positive thinking alone just won't do it. There are simply some things you've got to do after you've finished meditating and playing around with your creative faculties.

I used to spend my days giving everything I had to my removals company. Grinding day in, day out in this relentless pattern of "do the work once, get paid once". My blood, sweat and tears would testify that I had no leverage and that I was killing my true self softly. I'd go home shattered, and the time I took off at the weekend I felt I needed as recovery time. The last thing I wanted to do was fun family stuff and socialising with friends.

I felt that I had used up all of my energy, that I gave my business the best of me and my family got what was left of me.

I had no idea that I was electric and had the power to build up my energy from within.

Seeing is believing

Did you know that there is actually a way to see your energy? I'm being serious, I promise.

In 1939, Semyon Kirlian discovered, completely by chance, that if an object on a photographic plate is connected to a high-voltage source, an image is produced in it that appears to show the energy discharge around that object. Kirlian and his wife were convinced that their images showed a life force or energy field that reflected the physical and emotional states of their living subjects.

It just so happens that Kirlian photography shows that all humans have a glow that surrounds them which cannot be seen by the naked eye – an aura that shows humans are a ball of energy in a mass of vibration where everything moves and nothing rests.

Even when we're sleeping, nothing about us rests. Our heart beats through the night. Our lungs filter air in and out of us. Our eyes are flickering rapidly. Our blood rushes through our veins. The only thing that seems to rest is the one thing that can put us in a bad vibration: our consciousness.

I was raised to believe that sleep is something I needed to do to rest and replenish my energy levels, now I think of sleep as a spiritual practice.

For years, I had no control of the energy coming to me. How could I? I was not aware of it.

The energy moving towards me in my moving company was the anxiety my customers felt. Moving home is one of the most stressful things a person can go through in life, and there I was absorbing the energy being expressed by people in a bad vibration because they were stressed out about moving house. Anyway, enough about me.

Can you now see how plugging yourself into a rich vibration is what you have to do to become happy, healthy and wealthy? To initially shift your vibration means thinking differently. The goal is to get crystal clear on what it is that you want and flood your consciousness with it so a rich vibration becomes your default setting.

Your current default setting is not the finished you. It's just a reflection of how strongly you feel about the things in the world at this point in time. You can update your default setting any time you like. You have this power in your mind, we all do, but not in the part of the mind we actively use every day. In fact, it's the part of our minds that seems to quietly tick over in the background that has the power to make or break our success.

The most awesome thing to know is that…

# YOU ARE SUBCON- SCIOUS

I can imagine you're not entirely convinced that you *are* subconscious – you're probably thinking, "I have a subconscious mind, but that doesn't define everything about me." After all, we tend to think of our subconscious as being most active when we're resting. I'm not saying that you're asleep while you're awake, but I am asking you to entertain the idea that there could be a whole lot more going on with you than what meets the eye. You see, your subconscious (and mine, and everyone else's) plays a much more active role in your waking hours than you probably realise.

When you examine why you do what you do every day, you'll say this is the way you've always done things. You won't question whether there's a better way to do these things because what you're doing gets the job done. But this is where it gets interesting: why do you act in a consistent way every day? Why do you perceive other people overreact about something you consider a non-event? And why do some things scare you and other things excite you? And on it goes.

Here is another way to look at it: do you ever get a great idea, go to do it, and then suddenly something from inside scares the pants off you and you don't do it? You don't know where the surge of fear comes from or why you're suddenly bombarded with negative thoughts, and you revert back to what feels comfortable to you.

### Who The Hell Are You?

What is it that makes you do or not do what you do every day? What sends you signals in the form of gut feelings, fear and excitement? Ready for the answer? It's your subconscious mind.

But that doesn't tell you a lot, so I'll explain. There are two spheres of activity that beaver away in your mind: your conscious and your subconscious. This is the same for every person, and it works the same way for every person. It doesn't matter whether you're kipping in a bus shelter or you're residing in a penthouse; whether you were born into poverty or with a silver spoon in your mouth, every person's mind works exactly the same way.

In short, your subconscious holds all the answers you're ever going to need in life. It's so powerful that the world you see before you is what your subconscious has materialised for you, and on your say so. Your conscious mind is the device that sends thought waves through to the subconscious, just as I explained in the last chapter.

You may not be aware of it, but your subconscious has been working for you all your life.

Let's say, for instance, that you want to live somewhere new because you don't like where you live. Odds are this wasn't always the case. Cast your mind back to when you first found your residence. It caught your attention because it's just what you were looking for at the time, and you were delighted when it became yours. You were likely in high spirits and started painting it before you moved in so it was just right for you, and you enjoyed living there.

Basically, where you live now was once an idea you fell in love with. You attached so much positive feeling to wanting the house or the apartment that your subconscious accepted the idea and materialised it for you.

Another example could be your job or a business that you currently feel stuck in. Think back to when you first saw the advert for the job or the vision of the business, and notice how you got excited and started thinking of all the possibilities this new job or business would open up for you.

Again, the process is the same and the subconscious responds in the same way. The job or business you feel stuck in now was an idea you fell in love with in the past.

As time goes by, our wants and needs change. When you think about it, it's really not fair that all of the things we were once so grateful for and happy with catch the brunt of our mood in the present.

So take a look at everything you have in your life. Your car. Your home. Your TV. Your phone. Your clothes. Your socks. Your shoes. Your earrings. Your canvas pictures. Really look and you'll notice that most of the things you have are not things you need. So the question is, why do you have them? The answer is because you wanted them, and through your *thoughts*, *feelings* and *actions* you got them.

Let me give you a rundown of how your mind brings you what you want. Your conscious mind has the ability to accept or reject the thought energy coming its way from both the outside and the inside world. It can reason both inductively and deductively, meaning you have a choice. A choice to have a choice, if you like. If you're ignorant to how it works, your conscious mind is left in a deductive state which means it will pretty much make up its own mind on what to accept or reject, and it will do this based on your prior conditioning up until this point in time, as I explained in Chapter 3.

On the other hand, you can gain awareness and understanding and put your consciousness in an inductive state, which means you're in control. You can reason out the thoughts, ideas and suggestions that are flowing to you and reject them all if you want.

Now, there's no rule that you have to take control of what you accept or reject on a conscious level, but, like anything, it pays to put yourself in control of the thought energy that's coming to you so the right energy can flow through you. You don't want to slide backwards by allowing negative concepts to take root and flood you with terror and anxiety.

Another way to look at your conscious mind is that it's the intellectual side of you – the side of you that can think, choose and filter the good from the bad. Its greatest power of all is its ability to build pictures, any picture you wish to call upon. It can produce the ideals that you want there and then, even though your eyes haven't yet seen the physical results. New car. New house. New wardrobe. Holidays. The book you want to write. It can even see the you you're not being.

Whatever it is, your conscious mind can collate every last detail. It can put you in the new car, on the sandy beach or laughing with family and friends. It can take you out of your present environment and drop you into your ideal lifestyle.

The secret to the people who aren't seeing success is that they should start building their future now by building pictures in their mind. Like a time machine, you really can go back to the future and revisit these pictures to sharpen their form any time you like, and by doing so, you start impressing these pictures on to your subconscious mind.

This is exactly what you want to do because your subconscious mind has no ability to reason, form an opinion or think things through. It's deductive by nature and just accepts what you give it. Thoughts, ideas and suggestions that are repeatedly impressed upon it will be accepted by the subconscious mind.

### Fall in love with your future

Another way to look at your subconscious mind is that it's the spiritual side of you. It's your emotional mind. Any thought, idea or suggestion that's infused with enough feeling can and will be gobbled up by the subconscious mind. So the question is, how do you add feeling to the thoughts and ideas you're flirting with but haven't yet fallen in love with? Big hint there.

Well, in the same way you build an emotional connection with any person you spend a good amount of time with – the more time you spend with a thought or an idea, the stronger the emotional attachment will become. First you build the picture, then you build the feeling.

You build the feeling by going back to the picture. Repetition is mastery. Hold the picture of the good you desire on the screen of your mind. Zoom in. Zoom out. Colourise it. Cover every aspect of it. It's the easiest thing in the world to do. Just lie down somewhere quiet, close your eyes and let your imagination run wild. Find out what you really want and build it. I use the word "build", but really you're unveiling it because it's already there.

Famous composer Franz Schubert was asked how he thought up such great music and he replied, "I remember the music even though I or no one else has heard it before." He basically ratified the message in this book: that your magnificence is waiting within you. You don't need to find the answers in the outside world because you already have them inside.

Another example is when famous artist Vincent Van Gogh was asked how he painted such incredible paintings, he said, "I dream my painting and then I paint my dream."[15]

So, once you have an ideal (an idea you've fallen in love with), work with that ideal by magnifying it in your mind. Revisit it and take another look around. Take a tour of your ideal. Take yourself out of the present moment and catapult yourself to the forefront of your ideal. When you bring the future alive in the present moment, you're impressing everything you want on to the part of you that has no reasoning faculty, is totally deductive and knows only how to bring all the pictures it sees and feels into being in its physical counterpart.

"If you can see it in your mind you can hold it in your hand," is something Bob Proctor not only said but proved time and time again throughout his own life and the lives of his students.[16]

In 1968, he took out a pen and wrote that he would build a company that operated all over the world. He had no idea how to do it and didn't have the money to pull it off. The one thing Bob Proctor knew at

---

[15] *A quote by Vincent van Gogh* (no date). https://www.goodreads.com/quotes/17974-i-dream-my-painting-and-i-paint-my-dream.

[16] *Proctor Gallagher* (2015). https://www.proctorgallagherinstitute.com/if-you-can-see-it-in-your-mind-you-can-hold-it-in-your-hand/.

that time was that he didn't need to know how, because the how would be shown. So when you're thinking of a worthy ideal, it's not a question of how, it's a question of, "Do you want it?"

He wanted it, believed it would happen and his personal development company (Proctor Gallagher) grew to a size where his training could be broadcast all over the world. Anyone from anywhere with an internet connection could buy his products and have them delivered instantly.

Bob Proctor left us in 2022, but his company still operates all over the world in 2023 through his timeless books and recordings.

What can we learn from Bob Proctor? That if you can visualise your future, and truly believe in it, then it can be achieved. The trick is to impress only the pictures you want to move towards into physical form. Kick anything else out. You have the inductive reasoning to reject anything that doesn't fall in line with what you want to bring into your world. Impress the ideas you want to move into and form these into reality with faith over fear and love over hate.

Living with faith, love, passion, joy and excitement is paramount to your success because your feelings are the fuel. They can either be positive or negative: good or bad. When you feel good, you think good. When you feel bad, you think bad. It's simply not possible to feel good and think bad. So many people feel bad because they are locked into a negative vibration through the way they habitually talk, think and self-talk. It's all bad so they feel bad. In the same way thoughts are aligned to feelings, thoughts also trigger feelings. I've found that most people identify with negative emotions more easily. This is largely because most of us are used to negative thoughts and know the full extent of the negative emotions we feel – much more than the positive emotions. Practice is therefore essential, especially if you've not experienced many positive emotions growing up.

Protect your subconscious mind from negativity

Have you ever heard the expression "when the emotion is high, logic is low"? This is true due to the subconscious mind. I'm sure you've become angry with someone before and have totally lost it over a minute thing,

## Chapter 4: You Are Subconscious

only to regret it an hour or two afterwards. We've all been there.

You don't know what caused you to overreact like that, and you even start doubting your self-control.

Let me explain what happens. Energy is flowing to you all of the time: in this case, as a thought, idea or suggestion about something someone said or did. It came into your consciousness and you had the ability then to either accept or reject this energy. Invite it in and dance with it or kick it to the kerband be done with it.

Their act went against your beliefs, so you voiced your opinion or thought in strong disagreement and believed this was putting distance between yourself and the other person. But while a feeling in itself is an invitation, a strong negative feeling is a gatecrasher. It blunders into the party without thinking about or caring what havoc it causes along the way. This is what happens when you let negative emotions into your subconscious without first checking them. As soon as your subconscious accepts an idea, the energy is no longer flowing to you, it's now flowing through you and must be expressed. Uh-oh.

You have no control at this point because the energy has to be expressed through outward action. "But how do I prevent this from happening?" I hear you ask. Well, it all starts with the conscious mind. You must get on to the conveyor belt of your conscious mind and start living there so you can throw out the negative thought energy as it comes into you. Think of your conscious mind like the bouncer at your party: it can assess everyone coming in and choose whether or not they are allowed to enter – no gatecrashers here! You can stamp all negative thought energy with rejection there and then and part ways with each blip of negativity for good.

So when someone says you're not a very nice person, you don't have to feel disrespected and offended – you can use your reasoning faculty. You can roll this idea around in your conscious mind and ask yourself if that's true. You can think, I wonder why that person said that to me. Did I do something that upset this person? Is this person having trouble in their personal life and taking it out on me? I don't have to accept that; I'm actually a very nice person. With that, the thought is gone and you're not emotionally involved with a negative idea that could end up with you believing that you're not a very nice person.

This is how you control the flow of thought energy so you're sending only the thoughts, ideas and suggestions that you want to see in your life to your subconscious. This is essential because the subconscious mind is an emotional beast which cannot be tamed once it's been rattled. It's like a lion who's been grabbed by the tail.

Of course, even if a strong negative emotion sneaks in, eventually you calm down and cool off. However, you're left feeling embarrassed and remorseful; an inner pebble is thrown and you receive a chink in your self-image that makes you even more self-conscious than you were beforehand. Logic pokes its head around the corner and struts over as if to say, "I told you so." You end up muttering something to yourself like, "Next time I'll keep my mouth shut."

## Harness the power of your subconscious mind

On the flip side, your subconscious mind is an infinite storehouse of ideas, knowledge and power!

When an ideal comes to your mind that you've never achieved before, it's going to feel unnatural and far-fetched because you've never been to that place before. Naturally, doubt and worry are going to circulate and all of the reasons why you can't bring the idea to life are going to have a party in your mind.

The average person allows doubt and worry to gatecrash the ideas they fall in love with and they slip out of the backdoor of their consciousness as a result. They don't have the reasoning know-how to kick doubt and worry out of their mind so that faith and understanding can make themselves at home in their consciousness.

The person who knows who they are backs themselves with total confidence because they're aware of how powerful their creative faculties

## Chapter 4: You Are Subconscious

are, how the laws of the universe work and how their conscious and subconscious mind works.

They don't just believe; they know that where they are in life is an outside expression of the fixed ideas living in their subconscious mind. They also know that these fixed ideas are changeable. And by changing them, they know they can amend their environment, their bank balance, their relationships, their health and their entire world through doing this one thing.

They know that everything they need to succeed needs to be induced, developed and drawn out from inside. They know they're hooked up to an infinite source of intelligence that flows to them on a continuous basis through the form of ideas, thoughts and suggestions. They also know that by auto-suggesting their worthy ideals again and again through use of their conscious thoughts, feelings and actions, they're making an impression on their subconscious mind to get what they want to move into form and one day show up in their outside world.

This self-discovery gives you the power to create your own environment, and recreate it any time you want.

The conscious mind is where the work takes place. Your work. All things have to be formed in the conscious mind before the subconscious mind can form a physical replica. So it pays to watch your thoughts, watch your language and only feed your mind with the good stuff. The positive. The life you want. The house you want. The car you want. The relationship you want. So, what exactly do you want?

The conscious mind is the builder of all things. The chair you're sitting on, the car you drive, the clothes you wear were all once just a formless idea in someone's conscious mind. Everything around you was once a formless idea in someone's conscious mind. In most cases, a formless idea usually denies logic. It's only when its physical counterpart shows up in a tangible form that it defies logic and redefines it.

The Wright brothers were totally illogical when they set out to build a device to allow humans to fly. Their father, who was a very religious

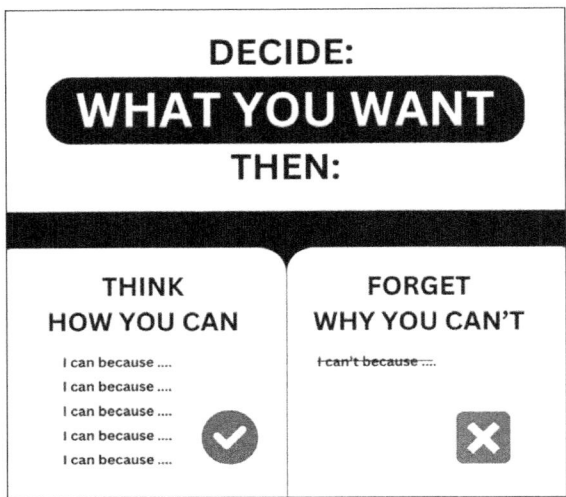

man, is reported to have said they were going to burn in hell for suggesting we could fly. No one at the time believed flight was possible for humans. It was totally illogical to suggest such a thing at the time because it had never been done before.

So all the Wright brothers had to work with was a formless idea that existed only in their minds. They had nothing else to draw on apart from the infinite source of intelligence they had within themselves. They couldn't compare their idea with other models of flying machines because there weren't any. It had never been done before. And yet, in 1903 they defied logic by achieving their goal of their first controlled aeroplane flight. In 1902 it was illogical for humans to fly in aeroplanes. In 2023, it's a logical way to travel. Where did this logical way to travel come from? The human mind. But it started as an illogical idea, and from fantasising with the imagination before that.

It wouldn't be entirely inaccurate to say that all greatness comes from fantasising. I'm sure that when Steve Jobs thought of the iPod, he was fantasising about putting entire catalogues of music in people's pockets. When Elon Musk thought of the reusable rocket, he was probably fantasising about a self-landing rocket. When you think about it, there really is no other source to pull from to create a new idea than the infinite source of intelligence you have inside of you.

It's not like the formulas for the iPod and the reusable rocket could have been pulled out of the Harvard business manual. They didn't exist in physical form so there was no "how to" to draw from on the outside world. In fact, that brings me to another thing worth mentioning – you don't need the "how to" when you're getting started. All you need is the "why to". Why do you want to do this? Why is it a good idea?

All greatness had to come from the infinite source within. If not from there, then where else?

I'm of the opinion that it pays to have a love affair with fantasy. Get the future well designed. Build the picture, then use your imagination to build the feeling so you can get yourself in harmony with what you're fantasising about by assuming it's true in the present moment.

Why? To get your subconscious working to your commands.

American author Neville Goddard wrote a great book on The Law of Assumption called *The Power of Awareness*. The one question he advised all people to ask themselves before falling asleep was, "Now my dream is fulfilled, how do I feel?"[17]

I invite you to ask yourself that question right now.

### Fall in love with positive ideas

What happens on your ideal day? What time do you wake up? What do you do? How do you feel? This is personal. All the ideas are within you. They're already there. This is the easiest work you can do. All you have to do is dive down and haul it to the surface. Most people's relationships with positive ideas are purely platonic – you want to make your relationship with positive ideas into a passionate love affair.

---

[17] Goddard, N. (2016) *The Power of Awareness*. Simon and Schuster.

I'm serious, by the way. How many bedrooms does your dream home have? What colour are the doors? Is it carpeted? What does the garden look like?

Here's the thing: two people can close their eyes and think of their dream home for 15 minutes. If you were to ask the two people to describe their home, you'd have two entirely different descriptions. That's because everyone is different. We think different thoughts. We want different things. One idea equals two pictures for two different people.

Your mind is an amazing piece of equipment you can call upon at any time; I dare you to give it a go. Lie down somewhere quiet for 15 minutes and see what you want to see, and see yourself in possession of it. Bring it all to life. Paint it all clearly. Sharpen the image. Outline it with black marker pen and then transfer everything on to paper in the form of writing and drawings.

You can accept or reject as you go, so bat the crap out of the way. It brings no good. Impress only the pictures you want to move into a tangible form because your subconscious is a careless doorman who just lets anything with a heartbeat into the show. This show is your life, so get involved.

You don't have to get emotionally involved with a destructive concept. All thought is neutral – it only "is" and will only ever be "is" unless you turn the "is" into the form of good or bad.

Your subconscious is a nodding dog to the ideas you feel, so don't flirt with negative concepts on a conscious level, and certainly don't fall in love with them. Kick all negative concepts that emit worry, doubt or fear to the kerb.

You can't let the outside world dictate your thinking. You have to go deep and get home.

That's why my dream home is called InsideOut.

I'm still unveiling it in my mind at the moment. Peeling back the curtains of each room by holding the thought on the screen of my mind through daily visualisation and then transferring the details on to paper through writing and drawing the creation.

## Chapter 4: You Are Subconscious

Once it's fully revealed itself to me on the inside world, it'll only be a matter of time before it exists in my outside world.

That's when other people are going to see it too. They're going to look at my house sign and say, "Why is your house called InsideOut?" I'll tell them it's because I saw it first in my inside world and I fell in love with it there long before it showed up in my outside world. InsideOut.

If you can take one thing from what I'm saying, don't let the outside world control you. Your present results (outside) do not indicate what future results (inside) you're capable of.

Even though the subconscious mind accepts what you tell it the most, it's vitally important that you develop a deep understanding that the wanting is in the conscious mind and the feeling is in the subconscious mind.

Isn't it empowering to know that you are permanently plugged into a device that has yet to be beaten?

If right now you're worried that you're walking around with not many good ideas about a lot of things, fear not. You can reprogram your subconscious mind in a number of ways through constant spaced repetition.

Not only can you form the ideal pictures in your mind and revisit them once a day and transfer the details on to paper until you have the full picture, you can also practise positive self-talk on a daily basis. Don't not accept self-talking badly about yourself or putting yourself down any more. Don't say, "I'm poor." Say, "I'm overcoming a cash flow problem." Don't say, "I'm so stupid." Say, "Well done for identifying a blind spot that can be worked on." Reframe the negative whispers of your inner nattering. It's so important. If you heard someone you know say some of the things you say about yourself, you'd be pretty upset with them and yet you allow yourself to talk yourself down on a daily basis.

What you say to yourself about yourself when you're by yourself is vital. What you're saying in your conscious mind is flowing straight into your subconscious mind, so it can prove to the negative Nancy in you how right you are about yourself. But that's crap.

You must take control of your self-talk and I recommend you apply the self-talk principles that Shad Helmstetter covers in his book, *What to Say When You Talk to Your Self*.[18]

In fact, I feel so strongly about this that I insist you buy a copy of this book, and as soon as it's in your hands, get your phone out, open up the voice memo app, press record and talk Shad Helmstetter's suggested self-talk into your phone.

The benefit of doing this is that you can listen to the recording every day to raise your vibration, increase your self-esteem and reprogram your subconscious mind. Hearing it back in your own voice is super powerful because you trust your own voice. Your subconscious has been taking orders from it forever.

Here's a taste of what you can expect:

*"I really am very special. I like who I am and I feel good about myself.*
*Although I always work to improve myself and I get better every day, I like who I am today and tomorrow, when I'm even better, I'll like myself then too!*
*It's true that there really is no one else like me in the entire world, there never was another me before, and there will never be another me again."*

The other thing you can do is choose one thing to do differently every day for a month. Then when you get to the next month, add another thing. The thing is, most of us are strangling ourselves by what we're doing every day. These are the things we're doing on autopilot.

As a human race, we love routine. It makes us feel safe. However, the trouble with feeling comfortable is that we'll always be comfortable but we'll feel stressed about it. We'll have our survival instincts like food, water and shelter covered, but we'll spend our whole lives worrying

---

[18] Helmstetter, S. (2017) *What to Say When You Talk to Your Self*. Simon and Schuster.

about it because we're just getting by. We're clinging to our food, water and shelter with our fingernails.

### Repetition gets results

You may think you're the one who's in total control, but you're not.

Your subconscious is the engine that's idling in the background of everything you do, driving your actions, whether you're aware of it or not. How well you tend to your subconscious is what determines how well it's going to serve you. If you're putting the wrong fuel into this hungry engine, it's going to fail you. If you're not watering it with the right thoughts, it's going to slow you down, burn out and overheat without your consent. The way you get in the driver's seat and take control of the accelerator is simple.

Crowd out your consciousness with all of the things you want. Spend all your time doing it.

Why? Because you can control your conscious mind and in doing so affect change in the subconscious that controls you. By thinking in a certain way (the way you have so far in your life) you programmed your subconscious. The good news is it's down to you to reprogram it by thinking in a new way. Even though it's in control of you, it's not like it's holding you to ransom. It may feel that way when you lack understanding, but in reality it's nothing more than a deep code that's been hard-wired through repetition. This means you can change it in the same way you built it, through repetition.

Repetition of thought and of action. This means not only thinking, but also doing things in a certain way. A way that is different to the way you've thought and done things up until this point. A way that is different to the way you've been shown by the people who raised you.

Touching on the people who raised you, they're important people in all of this inasmuch as you couldn't have possibly written the entire code of your subconscious yourself. You may have originated part of it, but, when you were a child, the code was largely written by someone else because your subconscious was wide open to all of the trivia that was going on around you. The deductive side of you that has no ability to reject was left defenceless. Absolutely everything that was going on around you was absorbed by your subconscious mind and, unless re-evaluated through your inductive lens, remains locked inside.

Therefore, the actions you take are in perfect harmony with your programming, even if it doesn't feel that way. I see so many people wanting to drop some pounds, eat healthily or get in shape, but they don't want to change the actions they take. They get frustrated and lose strength in themselves. With all of the will they can muster, they go on diets, off diets, on diets, off diets. They can't stick to the diet because of their subconscious mind. They don't realise what they're up against so they don't know how to outwit it.

Often, the good feelings associated with eating the bad stuff outweigh the bad thoughts that come with eating the good stuff. Hey, the bad stuff may even be associated with a reward. I remember as a child being rewarded with a bag of sweets and chocolate for doing something good. I'm not saying that's a bad thing. The feeling of love and warmth when someone buys you a gift is a wonderful energy that flows through you. It's just an example of how we attach a strong feeling to a thought that ends up in our subconscious. A feeling that's logged, lodged and works like a charm for eating the bad stuff, but wreaks havoc when it comes to only eating healthily. This leads to the behaviour that every time you do eat healthily, you reward yourself with a bag of sweets, chocolate or biscuits. This is very common.

I've found the three most impactful things you can do on a daily basis to keep your mind on track are making a conscious effort to improve your self-talk, performing success habits (like the ones I'm sharing with you in each chapter) and polishing up your ideals.

Easier said than done, right? Yes, because something unforeseen always happens and pulls you off track. I get it. But you don't need to master everything at once. You've spent decades doing what you're doing, so you can't expect to change overnight. You've got to give yourself a little time to adapt to the new improved ways of doing things.

**SUBCONSCIOUS SUCCESS HABIT/** For the next three days, write down everything you "say" to yourself. Use the exact words that come into your mind – don't doctor them to make them seem kinder. At the end of those three days, read them back to yourself. For each negative piece of self-talk, write down a positive alternative. Whenever you start with one of those negatives, swap it for one of the positives you've identified.

It all starts with awareness. Now you understand that you become what you think about, and that what you say to yourself, about yourself, when you're by yourself shapes your identity and how others see you, you'll start catching yourself talking yourself down in your mind. You can think, is that true? Because I don't need to accept that. Never again will you be able to slag yourself off with that same innocence. It's been clocked. You're on to it. You're on the path of positive change.

Now you know this, it's time to develop your awareness of why you, along with the rest of us, have continued doing the same things every day even though they're not getting us any closer to our ideals and the life we want to live.

Well, the answer lies purely in the fact that...

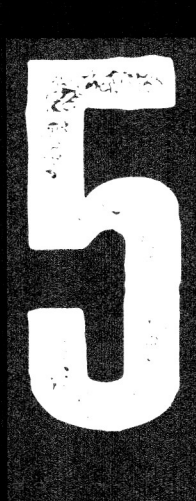

# YOU ARE HABITUAL

It's a well-known fact that humans are creatures of habit. We love our routines. So much so, we don't even realise that we live in them and that we shut ourselves off from all kinds of possibilities because they don't fit in with our habits. That's right, we'll stick with a habit even if it's doing us no good.

What makes habits so hard to change is that they're part of what is called our paradigm. The mental program that lives in our subconscious mind and has almost exclusive control over all of our habitual behaviour. Since almost all of our behaviour is habitual, if we're not getting the results we want, looking over our habits is one of the first places to check to see what the hell's going wrong.

As powerful and abrasive as they are, habits are elusive because they're things we do without any conscious thought. They're hiding in plain sight. No thinking is required. We've already internalised them from performing them over and over, which means our conscious mind is no longer involved. We just act without being aware that we're doing the same things every day.

When I first learned this, I found it eerie. I had a moment of realisation – I was not aware of most of the things I was doing every day. Spooked out and sceptical, I went about my days spying on myself. Peeking in on what I was doing with a slight increase in awareness, I learned that I was brushing my teeth with no conscious thought. Tying my shoes with no conscious thought. Making coffee with no conscious thought. The list went on.

However, there are times in our lives when we're painfully conscious of the actions we're taking, like when we first learn to drive a car. Remember that? I'm sure you were consciously engaged then (and if you don't drive, think of any activity you've learned that has required your complete and utter concentration). When you learned to drive, you were as alert as a seagull on Brighton Pier. You had to work hard to ensure your concentration didn't slip; you were vividly aware of your every movement before, during and after you made it. Why? It was a new behaviour. Your subconscious couldn't help you. Only your conscious mind could lend a hand at this point.

Think back to the first time you drove a car.

Seatbelt. Left foot on the clutch. Turn the key. First gear. Mirror check. Accelerator. Handbrake. Left foot easing off the clutch. Is it safe to go? Is it safe to go? We're moving! You weren't already programmed.

So, to take all of it in when you haven't done it before probably had you feeling pretty tired, doubtful and excited afterwards. The new behaviour set up a foreign vibration in your body, but you didn't let it stop you. Before you started, you probably thought it was easy to drive a car, then 15 minutes into your first lesson you were doubting whether you'd ever be able to drive a car.

But you kept at it. After a while of stalling, clutch riding and kangaroo jumping you started to notice that it got easier every time you drove the car. Easier to do. Easier to remember. After doing it over and over and over again, your new behaviour became familiar and you had to think less about what you were doing. The more competent you felt, the more confident you got. Through the repetition of driving the car, driving the car and driving the car, the day came for you to pass your test and you have never looked back.

The reason I'm telling you this is because I'm wondering, do you remember putting your seatbelt on this morning? Can you tell me how

## Chapter 5: You Are Habitual

many times you used third gear? The answer is probably no because you now drive your car by habit.

Did you brush your teeth in a different sequence today compared with yesterday?

What did you do first this morning, drop a spoonful of coffee in your cup or flick the kettle on?

See, all of these things are habits. We do them without any conscious thought, and we're all loaded up with our own set of habits. We've packed our day full of them. We behave in a certain way, every day, due to our habits, and what we do frogmarches us to our results.

### What's serving you?

Many of our daily habits serve us, many do not. The simple idea is to replace the bad with the good. Swap out the negative with the positive; the unproductive for the productive. I'm constantly on the lookout for my bad habits so I can replace them with good habits. I want new habits that make me feel good and nudge me towards the good that I desire.

So many great people are enslaved by a few bad habits that, if changed, would alter the course of their life in a rippling effect, so not only them, but the crowds of people around them benefit too.

Here's an idea – instead of watching the news tonight, read a few more pages of this book.

In my opinion, watching the news is one of the worst things a person can do. People in the habit of watching the news load themselves up with terror and suffer unpleasant days as a result. They feel downbeat and anxious about the world because of the negative energy that they allow to flow to and through them. They fill their consciousness up with all the latest news tragedies.

If they realised how their mind worked, they would never pay attention to the news again.

Impressing horrific ideas on to your subconscious through watching the real-life horror stories of the day is like dancing with the devil.

The mind is a broadcasting and receiving station that responds to ideas, thoughts and feelings. I suggest you avoid the news so as to not let your mind vibrate with the tragic, barbaric trivia of the day.

As simply as that, just by breaking the habit of watching the news, you can improve your life tenfold. Deep down, you already know this.

You also know full well that it's what you do in life that leads you to your results. You know it better than anyone. But the fact you know isn't enough to make the difference you seek. It's never what you know or the plans you make, it always comes down to what you do.

Knowing something on an intellectual level does not mean you truly understand it on a spiritual level. You'll know whether someone truly understands something on a spiritual level by what they do on a physical level. You just have to watch someone to know if they truly understand what they say or nod their head to.

It's not rocket science to work out that positive action leads to positive results, so if you continue to do things the way you've always done them, you're always going to have what you've always had. So if you're wondering where you're going to be five years from now, just take a look around because you're already there. No change simply equals no change. Oh, you're holding out for your income to take a lucky jump? Good luck with that.

I can't count the amount of hilarious people in denial who I've run into throughout my life: people who have told me the ins and outs of how to run a successful business, despite the fact they don't run businesses themselves. They never have. They always have that smug look on their face like they choose not to run a business because they're too shrewd for that game. This is an example of someone who understands how to run a business on an intellectual level, but doesn't on a spiritual level. How do we know that? Because their actions have led them to not be a business owner.

Now, not everyone wants to run a business for themselves. I get that. My point is that a person who tells a business owner how to run a business when they've never run one themselves is doing so through a lack of awareness and understanding. Kind of like all of the football supporters every Saturday who can't understand why one of their players doesn't score what they perceive is an easy goal. It's one thing sitting on the sidelines forming opinions, another thing to stay cool, calm and composed in a high-pressure situation.

Understanding can only be expressed through action: by taking the right action. This brings us back to awareness – you can't start taking the right action if you don't know what the right action is.

For example, every morning you wake up with something new to do, and this new thing always feels like the one thing that's hard work. It's taking up all your attention. You've got to somehow fit it into your day and you could do without it because your day is already full.

Why is that? Why can't you just mentally digest this one new thing into your day, thought free? Why does it feel like a struggle? Well, your entire day is already clogged up with your habits. That's why.

So, what are you doing every day? It's time to take inventory and keep tabs on yourself to avoid running around like a headless chicken.

How many hours do you spend indulging in unhelpful thinking habits?

### Flip your perspective

By way of an example, your car breaking down may feel like a bad thing, but there's a good in everything.

You may be rushing to get to an appointment and your car breaking down means you will now not make that appointment, which is a frustrating situation. But then let's say because you aren't in that appointment, you take an important call on your mobile phone from a troubled friend or family member and you make them feel better about themselves. When you next see them in person they thank you because they were feeling suicidal in that moment and your words changed their whole perspective. That's a good thing that would not have happened if your car hadn't broken down, because you would have been at the appointment with your phone switched off.

This is why you should always look for the good in bad situations; it won't always be obvious, but it is there. How do we know? Because everything has an opposite. So, the next time you send your child to school without their PE kit and you feel really bad about it, flip the script and find what's good about it.

How many times have you been in a bad spot, only to look back on it and say, "It's a good job that the bad thing happened when you think about it. If it hadn't happened, this good thing couldn't have happened afterwards."

That's just an example of finding the good from a bad situation after the event. But the good was always there. Sometimes you just have to look for it. Always looking for the good in things is a habit.

You don't need to live like a monk to form better habits and live a more peaceful, more productive and more disciplined life. People say things like, "It's all right for you, you're disciplined. I'm not." That's not true. Everyone is disciplined. Addicts are disciplined – so disciplined in fact that they turned what they were doing into an addiction.

The word "discipline" is grossly misunderstood. Most people have a vision of a stiff-upper-lipped army corporal inspecting soldiers. They assign discipline to people who have six-pack abs, impress army corporals or have a spotless home that smells of bleach. Here's all you need to know: a disciplined person is someone who can give themselves a command and then follow it. They make a commitment to completion.

You don't need to have your bed sheets ironed, your shoes polished, and be clean-shaven to be disciplined. This idea of discipline comes straight out of the army barracks. I'm not discouraging you to get some order, by the way. I'm just urging you to look at discipline in a warmer light.

An example of giving yourself a command and following it could be swapping the bottle of wine for a bottle of water during the weekdays. I'm not saying never have a glass of wine, I'm just saying that you can reason with the bottle before pouring.

Or come back to what I talked about in the last chapter – instead of talking yourself down, start talking yourself up.

Read a helpful blog that enhances your life instead of the social media newsfeed that makes you want to puke.

The name of the game is to flood your consciousness with the good that you desire so it's impressed upon the subconscious mind at all times.

### Think, then act

I'll say it again: everything you want is already here. It's been here all along just waiting for you to make contact. Once you've made contact through your creative faculties, you've taken a giant leap towards your ideals, but the failure to connect thought with action is the stumbling block to success.

You can only think and grow rich up to a point. Thought moves riches towards you. Action is where you take what is yours. The good you desire is yours. There's no question about it. There's also no question that it's your actions that determine whether you take it or not.

So this means acting in a new way, and acting in a new way is what halts a lot of people because it causes a foreign vibration in the body. When you're not aware of what's happening, the misfire of doubt and excitement makes you want to slide back into your usual vibration as soon as possible. However, I urge you to push through this foreign feeling, because it comes to all of us when we change the way in which we act.

Here's the thing: doubt sets up a fear vibration and is expressed in the form of anxiety, while excitement sets up a faith vibration, which is expressed through wellbeing. As I explained earlier, it all starts as thought energy. Both doubt and excitement are thought energy. The doubt originates from thoughts about what could go wrong, and the excitement from thoughts about what could go right. This takes us back to controlling the flow of our thought energy by using our reasoning faculty to make sense of the thoughts we think, and then deciding whether we want to accept or reject each thought.

Now, when you're moving forward into uncharted waters, negative thoughts are inevitably going to come to you because you've never done what you're trying to do before. So, this is where you earn your money playing gatekeeper to the thoughts that your subconscious mind wants to accept. You're also likely to have thoughts already in your subconscious mind which are working against what you're trying to do.

Ex-professional boxer Mike Tyson said he had this natural fear that he'd developed growing up on the streets and that he carried in his body as walked out to the ring, but he also said the fear was mixed with a new-found confidence and belief that was shown to him by a boxing coach who took him into his home and showed him a new way of life. The fear mixed with confidence he's talking about is a foreign feeling in his body.

The foreign vibration is best described as a misfire where you feel bouts of fear and anxiety along with bouts of faith and wellbeing.

Confused and uncomfortable, people want to feel how they normally feel so they stop acting in the new way and they end up back where they started – all because they lacked the understanding to ride the foreign vibration.

The foreign vibration will always pass. It's only present when you're moving into new territory. In fact, it's a great indicator that you're doing things the right way, if the right way to you is wanting to move forward.

I'm in a foreign vibration now. I'm writing this part while my book is in the pre-edit stage of the first draft. This means I've submitted a first draft to the experts who have read what I've written so far and have given it back to me to iron out a few vague points I've made.

So, even though I'm an author in my mind, to the outside world I'm not. I'm aware that while rewriting these parts, unwanted thoughts are coming to me which is causing me to feel and think things like, "I'm not cut out for this" and, "Just stop. You're not an author."

Even though I'm aware that my excitement for writing the book is wrestling with the doubt that I've never done this before, I still have to fight with myself to take action and keep writing. At times, everything in me is telling me to quit writing and revert back to packing up boxes and helping people move home.

Due to our beliefs and behaviours we want to hold on to what we've got, but we've got to let go and lose ourselves to find better things. We want to hold on to what we know works, even if it doesn't fulfil us, just because it's safe.

You're probably realising that who you've been thinking you are is not necessarily who you are anyway. So, it's time to have some fun with this.

Let's look at the facts. Most of your daily habits that consist of what you do, how you act and what you think have been passed down from someone else. It probably was passed down to them too. So, be conscious not to follow these footsteps, because you were made to create your own.

Know that something as seemingly minor as a habit either puts your neck in a noose or shoves you into the light.

We're born in a glorious vibration. We're free and then we're not.

We move through our little life and pick up all of these shackles that hold us back in our adult life, gift-wrapped and handed to us from people we looked up to when we're young. One of your family members says, "You can't do that," and so you think, "How could they be wrong?" and we believe them. That's a shackle.

Now, you've got to realise that most people don't realise how a throwaway comment can have such a devastating effect on a child and how it can stay with them through to adulthood. Most people are good people who are trying to pass on good things, but at some point you've got to start thinking for yourself.

That doesn't mean you blame the people from your past for your shortcomings in life so far. The past is the past. There's nothing you can do to change the past, so take the lesson and move on. Don't live out your days in the past – it's over. Let the dead bury the dead.

Always keep in mind that the right people want to see you glide through life with a smile on your face. So spend time around the right people. This is another renowned habit that will lead to success, as I mentioned in Chapter 3, when I covered how being around the right people controls the energy flowing to you. Don't spend too much time with people who are part of your past. Instead, spend time around the kind of people who are ready for your future.

So, regardless of your motive for picking up this book, you're reading this with all of these mental and physical habits that aren't entirely yours. The bottom line is if these habits have you out of tune with the good that you desire, you're nettled; you're tangled up in ideas that don't work for you.

"Cut the shackles that bind you to average," said Orison Swett Marden in his masterpiece *He Can Who Thinks He Can*![19]

The good thing to know is that I've found that habits to help you move forwards – like the success habits I'm sharing in each chapter – are the fastest and easiest thing to install when you add one new habit per month. No need to be a hero and add all the success habits in one day. That's too much of a quick shift. If you can do it, fair play to you, but I wouldn't recommend it.

> **EXERCISE: VISUALISE YOUR FUTURE/** On a daily basis, I do 15 minutes of visualisation. It took me a while to turn it into a habit because I would do it for a bit and then stop. Now, it's hard not to do it. Here's how I approach my daily visualisation time. I go to my bedroom during the day, lie on the bed on my back, set the timer on my phone to 15 minutes and then close my eyes.
>
> I think of nothing for a minute or two. Sometimes I'll check in with how my body is feeling, like whether my legs are aching from football training. I place my palms facing upwards, mentally take the tension out of my knuckles and I feel my fingers flop slightly. The aim here is to relax. But the

---

[19] Marden, O.S.(1908) *He Can who Thinks He Can, and Other Papers on Success in Life.*

last thing I want to do is try and relax; I want to let my body relax of its own accord.

Once I feel relaxed, I'll transport myself to my worthy ideals in my mind. This is the power of perception and imagination that separates us from all other lifeforms. Only you and I can do this. It's our own time machine, as I said earlier.

Often I'm driving up to the gates of my dream home, feeling the brake pedal under my foot as I'm coming to a stop to let the gates open. While I'm waiting, I check my rear-view mirror to see a quiet lane and a grassy bank behind me that I've just driven down. I catch a glimpse of myself from outside the car as if I were watching a film.

I then drive through the gates, reverse into my garage and the garage door comes down. Then I head through an inner door, turn left and walk past my utility room and into my state-of-the-art kitchen. My wife is cooking and my son is sitting on the sofa in front of a football match smiling at me.

That's my ideal visualisation, but what will yours be? Sitting on a tropical beach with a cocktail in hand? Walking into the head office of your successful business? Give it a go – all I'm asking is 15 minutes of your time.

These habits take time to install and they're not habits until you're doing them without conscious thought. It's all well and good performing new behaviours for a couple of weeks, but know that during that time you're doing them because you're consciously making yourself do them. This is exactly what you need to do at the start, but the fact remains that until you're doing them without conscious thought, they're not yet a habit.

Some say it takes 30, 60, or even 90 days to install a habit. I say it doesn't matter what the number is. If you're counting, you probably have the miracle cure attitude of, "I just have to find this one thing and I'm made," or you're thinking, "I tried that once and it didn't work for me."

## Attitude is everything

Do you know what trying is? It's called failing with dignity.

A good attitude gets you hitched up to an open mind that's flexible and able to adapt to unforeseen challenges and circumstances, whereas a bad attitude is a predetermined mindset that's rigid and closed to any form of outside reasoning. It's set in stone. So many people limit themselves by their attitude.

The reason it doesn't matter how long it takes to install the habit is because you have to install a habit with faith, and with the mindset that this is a new habit for life, not just for a month or as long as it takes to get what you want. After all, it's turning you into a slightly upgraded and modified you.

Maybe the first habit to adopt is the daily habit of improving your attitude. You may think you have a pretty good attitude already, and you're probably right. In fact you are right because whether you think you are something or not, you're right because that's what you think. But no matter how good or bad your attitude is, I can guarantee it can get better, and that is why "better" is such a great word – there is always room for improvement. Keep in mind that it's the small refinements upon something good that make it great.

That's why most people who want to affect positive change in their lives are looking for the special extras, the secrets, almost if there's a shortcut to the success they seek. They're looking to emulate the untypical traits of successful people in their field of pursuit, all in the hope that it will propel them to stardom. When that doesn't work, they feel deflated, as though they're doomed to the gloom they're surrounded by.

They've not considered that 95 per cent of success comes from the small things that are done well on a daily basis. The real "secret" is that successful people have mastered the small things that the average person overlooks and deems unimportant. Would you believe that 90s bad boy and Oasis frontman Liam Gallagher confessed to folding his clothes every night before going to bed. Who'd have thought?

Standard things like going to bed and waking up at the same time every day give you an enormous sense of confidence and stability. As tedious as it sounds, writing down six important things you need to do tomorrow increases your competence and productivity. As soppy as it sounds, showing affection and appreciation to your loved ones every day puts you and them in a wonderful vibration.

Meditating is a gift we can give to ourselves to calm down from the craziness of life. Exercising our body is a way to regain control of our physical body after we've been flung from pillar to post all day. Eating healthily and hydrating keeps our body happy so that it's working with us and not against us.

Please don't think I'm patronising you here. I know full well that you know all of these things are helpful, but you're not always committed to doing them. That's why I'm pointing them out. The difference is in the inches. A commitment to completion is the special bit; it's the razor-edge advantage that will make you feel invincible and skyrocket your results in all areas of your life.

You've seen people set out on the sea of new horizons by forming new habits. You listen to how fully committed they are to their new way of life, and you believe them because the moment they tell you, they are committed. A few days pass and they're lagging. The old habits are calling them. In a blink of an eye, they've stopped doing the new habits and are back doing things as they did before, and so nothing changes.

We've all been there. Maybe you're still there now. If you are, that's OK. Trust me. There is a way out.

When forming new habits, the trouble with using willpower and positive thinking to perform these new behaviours is not knowing what you're up against. You think you're just fighting your stubbornness and self entitlement, but you're not. You're fighting an unseen enemy. Your paradigm.

## Understand your paradigm

A paradigm is something we all have. You have one. I have one. The next-door neighbour has one. Your idols have one. Now, a paradigm is a mental program that has exclusive control over all of your habitual behaviour, and almost all of your behaviour is habitual, as we've established. This means if we want to change our results we have to change our paradigm. Our program of habits.

In order to take it on, it's essential to know how your paradigm was formed so you know the best way to tackle it. Your paradigm was formed through constant spaced repetition. That's to say, through the same thing happening time and time again, through you performing the same behaviour like tying your shoes or hearing the same phrase like your name.

Just think about your name for a second: if you had never heard your name before, someone could call it right now and you wouldn't flinch. You wouldn't even know what your name was. But due to your name being thrown your way over and over and over again, one day you started to respond to it, and now it's part of your paradigm.

What this tells us is that the way to reprogram a paradigm is in the same way that it was programmed originally: through repetition. I'm talking about doing the same things over and over again until your subconscious mind accepts it as part of your paradigm. With this new understanding of forming new habits, when you feel that resistance, you can intercept it by knowing that it's nothing more than your paradigm kicking up a fuss. Even though it feels like everything in you is telling you to quit, you can remind yourself that it's just your paradigm.

You see, the paradigm always wants to express itself the same way. In many ways, it's a great piece of kit to have. When you think about it, you're truly blessed to have your own automated system that's moving you towards the good that you desire. But here's the thing: it's down to you to make sure it's programmed to move you towards the good, rather than to maintain the mediocre or poor status quo.

## Chapter 5: You Are Habitual

I urge you to examine everything you do in the three hours after getting up from bed. You'll notice you're doing the same things day after day and you'll realise that you never paid much attention to them before. Some are helpful. Some are not. Washing the dishes is helpful. Checking your social media is not helpful. Enjoying the shower is helpful. Worrying about the workday is not helpful.

When it comes to the thought of changing your habits, the whole thing can feel incredibly complicated, like a minefield or an uphill battle you just won't win. Fear not, all you have to do is work in one new habit at a time. One new habit per month. Commit to that and you'll have 12 new success habits in a year's time, 24 in two, 36 in three and so on.

Don't complicate it. If you think drinking a smoothie every day is going to bring you closer to the success you seek, do you think you could drink one every day for a month? Sure you can. By the time you get into the second month, it's going to be hard to not drink a smoothie every day. We know that because habits are hard to break.

I wouldn't advise you to clutter up your mind by thinking hard about all the habits you should stop. You don't need to give any energy to those because it's pretty simple. You know exactly what you should stop doing, so just stop. Put your phone down in the evenings. Get off the internet. Don't eat the whole pack of biscuits. Again, just stop one thing at a time for a month and watch your life improve.

You'll find that your new behaviours that line up with the good you desire will raise your vibration to the point where your old behaviours fall by the wayside without requiring as much effort as you might have thought. Remember, the most effective way is to start slow and build momentum as each day passes. Rome was not built in a day, and 20–30 years of behaving in a multitude of certain ways is not all going to be altered overnight. But you can chip away at it, starting today and continuing every day moving forward. You must start now. This is the only time you have.

**HABITUAL SUCCESS HABIT/** Commit to the process of building new habits. I mean go all in – commit to changing just one small thing you do each day. Make that change every day for one month – no excuses, no "I can't today but I'll get back to it tomorrow." Commit, then act. At the end of that month, see whether you're consciously aware of performing that action. If it's become habitual, you're on the right track. Now commit to the next habit and keep going.

Everything you're seeking is seeking you. So, deep down, you know what you've got to do. You know you don't get what you want, you get what you are. But if you're anything like I was, I couldn't see how making small changes in my daily habits would illuminate my life.

Also, I didn't know where to start, so I'm going to give you five daily habit ideas that have worked wonders for me:

1 Drink one smoothie.
2 Write down ten things you're grateful for every morning.
3 Meditate for 5–10 minutes.
4 Exercise or practise yoga for 15 minutes.
5 Write down six things you've got to do tomorrow.

As you can see, these habits are not exactly earth-shattering ideas – but that's the thing: small changes in this area lead to big results. Positive habits make you feel good and give you the confidence to go after what you want.

Feel free to action my habit ideas that I've shared with you, but do them because you want to, not because you feel you have to or you should. If none of mine resonate with you, why not make a list of five of your own to get started with?

The power to change comes from within remember, not from outside. That's why it appears that so many people resist change. They don't resist change at all. They just resist being changed by someone else or because of something else.

## Chapter 5: You Are Habitual

If I decide you'll change, you'll resist that, and vice versa. But you'll see people who are set in their ways who one day decide they'll change, and to everyone's amazement, they change in an instant.

For example, one of my work colleagues told me that she happily smoked 20 cigarettes a day for 20 years, and despite her dad being a non-smoker and always telling her to give up, she didn't because she enjoyed it. What's interesting about this story is that when her dad died, she gave up smoking on the spot and now hasn't smoked for 22 years. She told me that if her dad were still alive, she's pretty sure she'd still be smoking.

Let's take money as an example. To earn an above-average income you must be an above-average person with above-average behaviours that stem from above-average habits. So don't just think, act.

You know you're already doing hundreds of things on a daily basis without any conscious thought, and as you're reading this you're becoming aware that almost all of your behaviour is habitual. More than this, you're now aware that your habits aren't you, they're just things you do on autopilot because, with the help of others, you've programmed yourself to do them. You can rest easy knowing that you can work in new habits any time that you like.

It all comes down to deciding what new habits to work in, and starting to do them over and over so the momentum builds and rewrites your paradigm until it becomes something you do without any conscious thought.

There's little emotion attached to working good habits into your day like writing your goals down once a day, pressing play on audiobooks or meditating for five minutes. Your only resistance will be your petulant thoughts, feelings and actions. Get over those by saying, "Do it now, do it now, do it now," in your mind. Or by saying, "I'll do it for two minutes and then I'm going to stop." Nine times out of ten, you won't stop after two minutes and you'll complete the habit, which is what you want, because excellence is a commitment to completion.

Now, when it comes to doing something new, and just the thought of it brings up fear, anger and a bad attitude, there's something deeper at play than just a mind-numbing everyday habit. You may feel dismissive, experience shortness of breath or even break out in sweat when put in certain situations, and therefore spend your life avoiding these scenarios like the plague.

This is where you think you differ from the world and that you're just not cut out for certain stuff. It has you thinking that you don't want to do certain things that you really want to do. The fear you feel in every pore of your body is clouding your thoughts.

This is down to the fact that…

# YOU
# ARE
# UNBELIEVABLE

If your dream is in conflict with what you subconsciously believe about yourself, you will never manifest your dream.

**Les Brown**

Les Brown speaks the truth. You can only attract what is in harmony with you. If you want to be a public speaker, but you hold the belief that speaking to a live audience is scary, then no matter what your fitness level, your fear will cause you to sprint away from the stage. Trust me.

The most rapid personal development exercise is swapping out your negative beliefs for positive beliefs. It's much more than just an oil change, by the way – this is a total restructure of your belief system. This isn't a case of positive thinking alone.

The truth of the matter is that most of your beliefs are not yours. You didn't originate them. They were passed down from family, relatives, and the friends of family and relatives. These beliefs were impressed upon you when you were a child, and not by force. You must always remember that your subconscious was wide open when you were a child, so you took things in like a sponge. You never evaluated them then, and you probably haven't evaluated them since – as I said in the last chapter, it's not your fault, and not the fault of the people around you.

The politics of it are irrelevant. The past is gone and there's absolutely nothing you can do about it; you can't change a goddamn thing about it. The past is an amplifier of your feelings about it and raking over old graves does nothing more than intensify your resentment. If you must look back, bathe yourself in the good memories and soak up the gratitude from those moments. Don't look back in anger, or forward in fear, but around yourself in awareness.

### Examine your beliefs

Now, without meaning to contradict everything I've just said about not looking back, dipping into certain points of your past to restructure your belief system is essential. If you don't, you're left with all of these negative, untrue beliefs that you didn't originate, and that you've never even evaluated.

Inherited beliefs that were plonked into your subconscious by other people years ago but live with you now.

I vividly remember this one time when I was 12 years old. I felt all grown-up because I correctly answered a couple of questions that had puzzled the adults in conversation. Then, out of nowhere, one of the adults shot me down in flames by saying, "No one likes a smart ass."

This made me feel small, powerless and totally disconnected.

I was a kid. Who was I to question an adult? At that moment I installed another person's belief that went, "No one likes a smart ass," which limited me for 30 years. In a split second, the outgoing 12-year-old reduced himself to an introverted person for 30 years. To a person who held back on speaking up and adding value in conversations, all because of one careless remark from an adult who should have known better.

Another time I won a game of pool against an adult I respected. After the game, someone asked how the game went, and the person who I had just played rolled their eyes and sarcastically said, "Ant won. He always has to win."

### Chapter 6: You Are Unbelievable

The petulant behaviour of this adult caused the 11-year-old me to originate a belief of my own that went, "I upset the people I love when I win."

Again another belief that limited me for over 30 years. Once the 11-year-old on a ruthless winning streak and destined for greatness, then a talented person of 30 years who never quite got over the finish line because he lacked the minerals. The nearly man with no killer instinct and who never quite made it.

So, what is a belief?

Well, a belief is an idea that is fixed in the subconscious mind. It's something you hold to be true. I'm not saying it is true, but it's an accepted concept that you hold as true. There are two types of beliefs: limiting beliefs and empowering beliefs.

Our limiting beliefs are caked in fear and both protect us and hold us back. Our empowering beliefs are laced with faith and push us forward.

Beliefs are laced with emotion, and when they identify with a present event, the same feelings rush through your body. This is why people get triggered again and again. The belief is running on autopilot: that's how all of us have the emotional baggage that we carry. It's not because there's something inherently wrong with us. It's because something once happened to us.

The next time you think to yourself, "What's wrong with me?" instead ask the question, "What happened to me?"

The first question makes you feel out of sorts and like you don't belong. Naturally, you're going to search for your defects and you will find them in abundance because you're looking for them. You're using your reasoning faculty in a destructive way by allowing it to cast its own direction.

The second question is where you will find the answer. It's important to know that we install our deep-seated beliefs through a significant event that happened to us. It's like a lingering afterthought that festers; that bitter taste that stays in your mouth. These types of beliefs you kind of originate, but then again, you don't.

To explain, let's say you're a 35-year-old introvert who gets social anxiety when you're speaking to a group of people. This is not uncommon.

What is uncommon is someone with the awareness to take the time to evaluate this situation and scratch beneath the surface.

When asked about it, you'll probably go down the highway of what other people say, like, "I don't like all their eyes on me," or "I don't like talking too much," or "I don't like being the centre of attention." Why?

What happened to you? What negative event happened in the past that warped this part of your character? You weren't born shy, self-conscious or with any of the labels you're giving yourself about talking to a group of people, so what happened to cause you to think this way? This is where you find the answer.

> **EXERCISE: UNCOVER YOUR LIMITING BELIEFS/** If you close your eyes and ask, "What happened to me?" a moment from the past will flash up in your mind. It may be seemingly insignificant, but it's not. If it flashed up in your mind first, this is a significant life event for you, so work with this moment.
>
> Next, you use your perception faculty that is like a time machine and transport yourself back to the moment in your mind. Sharpen the image and get the exact words or actions. You're wanting to find the energy that flowed towards you in that moment.
>
> Watch it as though you're watching a movie, feel it and you will begin to understand the origin of your limiting belief.

Let's come back to the example that you get social anxiety speaking to a group of people. If you did that exercise, the memory that flashed up for you may be that you were watching tennis on the TV with your older sibling and their spouse, and because tennis is your favourite sport, you were talking about it passionately, and then your older sibling said something like, "Cor, you're such a chatterbox, just like mum." This energy is received and sets up a vibration in your body.

The next day your sibling tells you that their spouse was getting annoyed at how much you talked during the tennis and it upset their evening. Young, confused and only meaning well, you installed the limiting belief: "I upset the people I love by talking a lot." OOOSH!

You find as you grow up that you're always uncomfortable talking to two or more people at the same time. You get hot, sweaty, say very little and find the whole thing overly complicated. You're ready to bolt out of there the first second you can.

As a result, you grow into an adult with a laden heart who struggles to form loving relationships and moves through life feeling isolated and alone. All because of this so-called "non-event": a non-offensive line of communication from your sibling that could have been laughed off had you known how the mind works.

That was 30 years ago. It's not fair on yourself to be limited when making friends and connections by something that happened 30 years ago. Therefore, the belief has to go.

It's great work when you find the moment, by the way. You always work from the root cause, so congratulate yourself every time you find the root cause to a belief, because now you have the details at your disposal.

If, however, nothing immediately springs to mind, you're going to have to evaluate yourself further. This is another habit for success that you can build. You'll find that if you get in this habit, the more you evaluate yourself, the more you're going to believe in yourself.

The bottom line is something that happened in the past that carried with it a huge emotional surge and implanted the belief in your subconscious mind. Every time a similar event or scenario emerges in the present, your subconscious goes into overdrive trying to determine what it means and will liken the present moment to that emotionally charged event in the past and flood your body with the same chemicals you felt way back when.

I've heard people say that your beliefs live in your body. I believe they live in the subconscious. When triggered, the sudden rush of uncontrollable emotion just feels like it's in every part of you, as though this is just the way you were raised and you can't do anything about it. Like you have a chemical imbalance. Your beliefs may cause a chemical imbalance in your body when they're rattled, but they stem from a past event.

Once you've got a past event to work with, you can investigate. You can inquire whether this belief has any semblance of truth. I'm going to furnish with you my belief-busting formula, so you're able to slash your limiting beliefs to bits, release the tension and twist your limiting beliefs into empowering beliefs.

When I find a limiting belief and I write it down on paper and read it back, my first thought is usually, "This is absolutely ridiculous." Yet, I wasn't thinking that while it was in my head running on autopilot.

**EXERCISE: HOW TO BUST YOUR LIMITING BELIEFS/** Follow this process to bust your limiting beliefs to pieces.

Answer the following questions in order – write them down, I find this helps to solidify my thinking:

1. What is the limiting belief?
2. Is this 100 per cent true?
3. Who are you with this belief?
4. Where does this belief come from?
5. What is the secondary gain of this belief?
6. What are the long-term implications of holding on to this belief?
7. How can you turn this around?
8. What is your new belief?
9. What action will you take to cement your new belief and release your limiting one?

When you're doing this process, you must put your ego to one side and be totally open. You owe it to yourself to drop the bravado and let yourself get involved with finding out who you are. You must be fearless, thorough and honest because it's only the truth that can set you free.

## Face your past to find your future

You might be done with your past, but your past might not be done with you.

You could be strutting through your days being totally unaware that

## Chapter 6: You Are Unbelievable

you're carrying a plethora of outdated beliefs with you. Beliefs that are helping you. Beliefs that are hurting you. All culminating into your very own invisible belief system that controls your decisions. Your belief system is how you see the outside world and, more importantly, how you see yourself.

Now, if you're thinking this is an irrelevant part of the book, think again. This could well be the most impactful chapter you're ever going to read in your life. I don't say this next phrase lightly. I mean every last word of it to my trembling core. Read it slowly, come back to it and reread it.

Your belief system is the forecast of your future. If you leave your belief system untouched, you cannot grow on an emotional level. Your inside world stays the same so your outside world stays the same. How sad. You have all the talent and ability you need to live the extraordinary life you were born to live, and yet you risk living an ordinary life because of the set of outdated beliefs you hold, which you probably did not originate. The most harrowing part of it all is that you may not even know it. You may not know you've inherited a lorryload of false beliefs.

To explain, your beliefs are so deep-seated that the average person doesn't even know they have a belief system, let alone how it works, or that they have individual beliefs about various things. But we all have them. They live in (you guessed it) our subconscious mind.

We have beliefs that limit us, hold us down and protect us from danger. We have beliefs that set us free, thrust us forward and leave us fearless. Beliefs about love, family, money, sport, religion, business, friends and travel. You name it, you probably hold a belief about it. And to think, it's probably not even yours.

It's just plain wrong to be lugging around other people's beliefs as you move through your days making things happen. As you run into life's ups and downs, someone else's negative beliefs can slash your character to bits, ruin your relationships and lead you to the depths of despair in a devastating way.

I'm not saying all of the beliefs you hold are not yours or that they are all limiting, but, just like your habits, a large part of your belief system was built by someone else. So whether they're your beliefs or someone else's, when initiated, the beliefs you hold can switch you from mood to mood like a remote control. You need to know your way around this area to get a grip on it.

Let's do a little exercise now. Cast your mind back to the story I told you earlier in this book about my 40-year-old friend who committed suicide. You can recall that story and you remember it so well because it's laced with emotion – and it's emotion that moves people to action.

Now, for my friend to get into a mental headspace that he was doing his wife, his three children and all his family and friends a favour by him not being here, a lot of negative thoughts were in his subconscious. Some of them were new. Most of them were old – old thought patterns and beliefs playing out unconsciously day after day that had him firmly convinced that ending his life was the best possible solution.

I believe that if my friend had known more about himself, how his subconscious worked, how his habits were formed, how his beliefs were responsible for all of his unconscious responses to life and that he could change them, he would have understood why he was feeling so low and would have unpicked his way out of the dark and into the light. I believe this because he loved a challenge. I don't think for one second that he would have left his family thinking "why?" and "what if?" if he knew more about himself. He'd have moved himself out of pain and into peace. He'd have found a way out that brought smiles to his children's faces instead of tears.

Through not knowing, he allowed traumatic events from the outside world to flow into his consciousness in a way that caused him to doubt and worry. This would have set up a vibration of intensified fear in his inside world that frightened him. With his world seemingly crumbling around him, and without understanding what was happening inside himself, he probably couldn't have seen the potent shots of anxiety he was suffering from ever subsiding.

I believe if he had known himself better and had the mechanical know-how of how to restructure his belief system, he would still be with us today. Of course I'm speculating, but knowing my friend as I did, I believe this to be true.

Please share this mechanical know-how with as many people as you can because I feel that everyone should have this method at their disposal. Give them my process for busting limiting beliefs. It's a beautiful system that can be done just with pen and paper, which is helpful for people like me who don't always feel like talking and would rather spend time alone making sense of the nonsense.

**You control your future**

The great thing to know about your beliefs is that, even though you had a little help from your friends and family, you, and you alone, signed them off. You may not have assembled them all, but you can dismantle them all. They may feel siff, static and cemented into your core, but they're not.

Not only can you show your limiting beliefs the door, you can also usher in empowering beliefs as a replacement. These empowering beliefs can redirect the emotion and lift your energy in alignment with the good that you desire.

Once identified, you can say, "Hey, Mr Limiting Belief. I want to thank you for looking out for me all these years, but the time has come for us to have a little chat."

Let's clear one thing up about limiting beliefs – you may not agree with them, you may be smarter than them and don't be at all surprised if you *think* you don't actually *believe* some of the things you do believe.

I've lost count of the amount of limiting beliefs that I've found in myself that I thought, "I don't believe that. I've gathered enough information, read enough books and been to enough seminars to know this isn't true, so I can't believe that," but I did.

It's only confusing when you don't realise that thinking is on a conscious level and believing is on a subconscious level. Just because you can intellectually think you don't believe something does not mean you don't actually believe it.

If you're on the fence about what you believe, go and meditate for five minutes and then ask, "What belief is blocking me?" Let your question sit in the silence. The answer will always come. When everything is calm, it's as though your conscious mind is tranquilised to the point where your awareness is heightened and you can reach the infinite intelligence that's within you.

It was an eye-opening experience when it dawned on me that I held a limiting belief about something I had enough information about to know it wasn't true, but it showed in my results.

The belief I found was, "You have to really work hard to earn lots of money."

Here's the thing: I saw people around me not working hard and earning lots of money, and I grew up around people who worked really hard and did not earn lots of money. Of course, I was told I had to work hard to earn money, so that's what I believed until I was 30.

I was 30 when I started getting business coaches, buying self-help books, investing in online personal development courses and going to seminars. It was in this environment where I learned that you don't have to work hard to earn money.

It made perfect sense to me. I knew there was something iffy about the belief. But back then, I didn't know I had beliefs that made me act a certain way. "You have to work really hard to earn lots of money," was just a saying to me, I hadn't realised I was subconsciously agreeing with it.

As a result of my personal development study, I no longer agreed with the saying. Brilliant. I'd finally dropped into an environment that talked my language.

But I continued working like a nutter to earn peanuts for another four years. If you had asked me if I believed you have to work really hard to earn lots of money, I'd have told you no. I would have told you

## Chapter 6: You Are Unbelievable

why and have given you a whole list of reasons why you don't have to work hard to earn money. I could have explained it in such detail that you would have believed me and I'd have convinced myself. So, why was I still working hard just to earn money?

I remember meditating one day and asking myself what belief was blocking me, and "You have to work really hard to earn lots of money," kept coming through loud and clear. I remember trying to deflect it because I thought I didn't believe it, but I did, and the evidence was in my results. I was really confused afterwards and felt that I really didn't know myself at all.

That's the thing: you can believe something on a conscious level, and yet your results would indicate that you'd never even heard of it, because you still believe it deep down on a subconscious level. You may believe you can make a lot of money but your results are showing that you can't make enough to pay your bills, all because the belief hasn't made its way down to the subconscious level yet. When you feel this way, go back to the myth-busting process. That's what I did.

Our belief system is our very own internal construction of the world that comes with guidelines, limitations and warnings to keep us safe. It's to keep us safe that we look at change as dangerous, which causes us to be afraid of leaving our comfort zone and trying something new.

So far, I've given limiting beliefs a bad press, but they're not all bad.

For example, I have a limiting belief that, "Taipan snakes are vicious, deadly creatures."

Now, I'm sure the people in the world who have way more understanding about taipans than I do will say that's not true. That's OK. I'm happy to remain ignorant in this subject and hold my belief as true for me. I've got no intentions of French kissing a taipan snake. If I did, I'd have to address my belief.

This is a prime example of how limiting beliefs can serve you very well in the right areas.

Another scenario would be wanting to give up or ease up on drinking alcohol because you can't deal with the hangovers any more. Limiting beliefs like, "Alcohol gives me headaches," "Alcohol upsets my stomach," and "Alcohol makes me feel anxious the day after drinking it," are all helping you to limit your alcohol intake. They're reinforcing your efforts and willpower.

You can use these as a launchpad to create new empowering beliefs to add a little more twist to the knife in order to kick the habit for good.

## We all need to change our belief systems

As you move through this process, don't give yourself a hard time here or start thinking less of yourself for holding on to all of these limiting beliefs you're about to run into. You put them there to keep you safe. They're protecting you, they want the best for you and they have served you well up until this point. However, when you start running into them, you're going to find many that are going to astonish you because they are utterly ridiculous. In the light of truth, you'll find that most of your beliefs don't even make sense.

A worthy mission in life would be to flush out all of the beliefs that are holding you back. The ones that are frustrating you and you don't even realise it. You owe it to yourself because they're standing in your way, and you have the power to destroy them.

I don't care how much information you get from books, seminars and online courses, without rewiring your belief system, you will never make the gains that you want to make.

You could pay for the latest business tips, tricks and strategies, and put the work in to implement all of them, only to find that you either can't do them or they won't work for you. Why? Because your beliefs are blocking you.

Unless you change your story about yourself, your story will always be the same.

Make no mistake: your life today is the story you believe about yourself.

## Chapter 6: You Are Unbelievable

You don't get what you want in life. You get in life what you are. So, we come back to that interesting question again: who the hell are you?

As a business owner struggling to get any handle on my team, I read all the books on recruitment, management and leadership to improve my skills and increase the productivity of my staff. I got frustrated at only making marginal gains, because I couldn't understand for the life of me why I couldn't galvanise them.

Never did it cross my mind that a limiting belief that I installed when I was 12 could be the cause of all the firefighting, but it was. I held the belief, "People will always let me down."

Wow! Because I held this belief, I was vibrating on a frequency that made me attractive to the people who would let me down, I employed them, and they continually let me down.

While the recruitment, management and leadership skills were useful and a requirement of my position, they were not the solution to the problem. The solution was a restructure of my own belief system in this area.

You see, what I was doing was what I trained to do: namely, to snatch a solution from the outside world. But the solution existed in my inside world. I thought I needed to improve my management and leadership skills, as though I was lacking.

That wasn't the case. I was starting to understand what Jim Rohn meant when he said, "Success is not something you pursue, it is something you attract by the person you become. So instead of going after it, you stay, and work on yourself."[20]

After working with a coach, I now use the writing formula I've shared with you in this chapter to change all of my limiting beliefs whenever they come up. And yes, in case you're wondering, they still come up.

To come back to the example I just shared, once I changed the belief to, "The right people will always be there to help and support me,"

---

[20] Money Motivation (2023) *Empower Yourself: Strategies for taking control of your life.* https://www.youtube.com/watch?v=nhE3luyPN0c.

everything changed within a week. To my amazement, the wrong people started handing me their working notice. They were having a hard time telling me. I was delighted.

They are great people, by the way. I was the one with the problem.

So, if you believe, "People are problems," it's highly likely that you'll have only a few friends, avoid parties and like your own company. That's OK if you're truly OK with that. But if the belief has been set up as a result of some past trauma to protect you from feeling hurt again, it would be wise to confront this belief and see if you want to keep it.

If you were brought up in an environment of a lack of money, this is likely to have filtered into your subconscious. Maybe you heard your parents always rowing about money. If they constantly said, "Making money is hard," then it's likely you will end up with that belief through hearing it over and over as a child.

This was long before you were out on your own in the world to form your opinion, so your subconscious mind accepted it as truth. We've all done it, because when we're a child our subconscious mind is wide open and all kinds of beliefs end up in there, but they don't have to stay there. As I've said, most of them need raking out.

That's a hard thing for most people to understand though. They think they're the way they are because that's just the way they are, but it's simply not true. Thinking, "This is just who I am, I can't be changed," is nothing more than a limiting belief. It's utter nonsense.

You are the highest form of creation on planet earth and have the mental faculties to recreate yourself any time you want. You don't have to stay the same person. You could be in a prison of your own making. Here's the crux of the issue: you can't escape a prison if you don't know you're in one. That's why awareness is very important.

**UNBELIEVABLE SUCCESS HABIT/** Use the exercises I've shared in this book to examine your belief system and uncover the limiting beliefs that are holding you back. Sounds simple, doesn't it? But I know it's not easy. The habit is in recognising when you're not getting the results you want despite following all the advice you've *consciously* taken onboard. That's your cue to step back and dive into your subconscious mind, because this is where you'll find the answers.

Here's an example to get you started.

**Limiting belief**
"I'm no expert on life anyway!"

**Is this 100 per cent true?**
No, even though I'm relatively young, I've got a wealth of life experience through having a son at 19, being a business owner at 23 and having a wife with breast cancer at 34. Added to that, being a homeowner and an investment property owner makes me well versed in many things a lot of people never experience in their lifetime. Things like responsibility, maintaining meaningful relationships and all things business.

**Who am I with this belief?**
I hold back on what I feel I should say in case the other person takes it the wrong way or in case I come across as arrogant. I don't want to breach someone else's values or upset them in any way. I also don't want to end up arguing with people if they don't accept my views.

**Where does this belief come from?**
It comes from conversations I had with certain adults who I trusted when I was growing up. They shot me down in flames by challenging my views and making fun of me. Not having a response for them made me feel small, powerless and not clever enough. This knocked my confidence in conversation for six. It was much safer to stay quiet and present myself as modest or unsure of myself.

**What is the secondary gain of this belief?**
It's the perfect excuse to hold back and always say, "Oh, I was going to say this important thing to help and make things clear, but I didn't in case it offended them in some way." Almost like my views are too good for this world. What a shame.

**What are the long-term implications of holding on to this belief?**
I'll never fulfil my goal of bringing more health, wealth and happiness to people's lives through sharing my findings with the world. This would make my life a resounding failure because I'd have no legacy to leave. This will make me feel weak, unhealed and sad because I never had the balls to tap my potential. I cannot bear the thought of looking back on my life like it was a worthless existence that held so much promise that I was too scared to pursue.

**Turnaround 1**
"I am an expert on life!"

**Is this 100 per cent true?**
Well, I guess every person is an expert on life in the area in which they spend most of their time.

**Turnaround 2**
"Other people in my field are experts on life!"

**Is this 100 per cent true?**
Not 100 per cent true. They are just like me, sharing their findings with the world in their own words to build connections, influence people's lives and profit in business. Other people are no more of an expert than me in my field.

**What should the new belief be?**
"I am an expert on sharing my findings with the world with the intent

of bringing more health, wealth and happiness to other people's lives."

**What would someone with the new belief do?**

1  Offer people in need helpful advice
2  Write a book

> A man who views the world the same at 50 as he did at 20 has wasted 30 years of his life.
> **Muhammad Ali**

The difference between you and that successful person you admire isn't that they know more than you. It's not that they're better than you. The difference is that their belief system is aligned with whatever it is that they're successful at.

People are all essentially the same. It's our results that are different.

We've been programmed to the hilt through our childhood, our culture and our class; the belief-busting process is our chance to unpick that programming.

You'll always find your limiting beliefs nestled behind the areas in which you feel you lack power. So, just think, where are you lacking power? Where are you not making the progress you know should? Where has your progression ground to a halt?

In a nutshell, you have limiting and empowering beliefs. Limiting beliefs limit your power, hope and progression in reaching the good that you desire, but they do serve you well in other areas by protecting you from danger. Empowering beliefs come with unlimited power, hope and progression in reaching the good that you desire.

The trick of life is to replace the limiting beliefs that stunt your progress with empowering beliefs so you're open up to receive the good that you desire.

All of this energy needs to be redirected to your inside world, and the results will show up in your outside world. However, with all of this invisible energy flowing towards you constantly, it can get confusing. When everything feels as though it is happening too fast, you may want to shout, "Please slow the energy down," but that's impossible. The reason why it's a challenge to process all of the energy that flows to and through us is because…

# YOU ARE INSENSITIVE

So far in this book, I've rambled on about the marvel you can create through the conscious use of your creative faculties; in particular through the use of your will, where you can hold one thought upon the screen of your mind to the exclusion of all outside distraction.

With the gift of your limitless imagination and your precise perception to create dazzling pictures in your mind, you can almost shut down your five physical senses and bring your mind in perfect harmony with the idea you're focused on. That is the hidden treasure you're blessed with.

But to exclude our physical senses and the outside world completely from this book would be a crime. To turn a blind eye to the everyday events that happen in life would be a total cop-out of my part. I want to help people who want to help themselves. I don't want you to have a "heard it all before" mumbo jumbo spiritual book sitting on your shelf that doesn't translate into the whirlwind of the day to day.

My goal is to spark your awareness of who you are so you're able to take actions that make a difference in your life.

Since it's your physical senses that are the faculties that enable you to communicate with your material world, there's no way that I will pretend they don't exist or they don't play a vital role too in finding out who you are and moving towards the success you seek.

Yes, it's your creative faculties that enable you to connect with a world you're unable to see with your eyes yet, and to visualise the ideal world you were previously unaware of but that you are now able to see in your mind. It's also true that it's this connection through your creative faculties that enables you to create the world as you want it.

However, that doesn't mean your physical senses are useless or have no role to play. Even though I've alluded to the opinion that our physical senses are our lowest mental tools, you can train your five senses to respond to the pictures you hold on the screen of your mind. In training your senses in this way, you'll cause them to spark like a lighter that doesn't ignite into a flame the first time you try it, but that shows enough of a spark that you can see there is life there that's ready to connect. All you have to do is spark that lighter a few more times.

Our physical senses of sight, smell, taste, sound and touch are easy to relate to because we know them so well, but there's always more than meets the eye. So, let's delve into them, have a mooch about and see what new insights we can find.

## Reacquaint yourself with your senses

Used on a daily basis to navigate our way through the day, the five senses put us in touch with the physical world and reality as we know it. We shake someone's hand, give them eye contact, smell their deodorant, hear their voice and we have a taste in our mouths the whole time we're doing it.

By now you know humans are habitual creatures and you are aware of exactly how habits are formed, so you won't be shocked to learn that our habitual traits determine the usage rate of our physical senses, which, when you think about it, shapes our character. I'm sure you're familiar with the notion that what you don't use, you lose; but the polar opposite is also true: what you use most, you get good at; what you use all the time, you turn into a habit.

We also know that if we lack one sense, our other senses can be heightened – a blind person will often have much sharper hearing, or a deaf person will be far more observant than those of us who can both see and hear.

I don't mean that if you don't listen, you'll suddenly go deaf, or if you're unobservant you'll become blind, but in both those instances it's fair to say that you're not using those senses to your full ability. However, if you were to listen more intently or become more observant as you move through your life, you would uncover new opportunities and improve your relationships.

### Communication: a case in point

In the case of communication, you and everyone else in the world have a habitual way of communicating. Your default will likely be the way you would prefer others to communicate with you. However, there are many different kinds of communicators in this world. What if you could switch the way in which you communicated, depending on who you were communicating with? You would level up in many areas of your life. Knowing how to communicate with other people by using their modality to converse with them is a sure-fire way of getting your message across, getting yourself heard and forming closer relationships.

How many times have you felt ignored or disrespected by someone not listening to you? The issue is usually not that they didn't listen. Instead, it's that they didn't take in the information. You may feel disrespected and devalued, but that's just an idea you've made up. The fact that you think the other person thinks you're not important enough to listen to is your problem, not theirs. And in most cases it's not true. You suspect their arrogance and yet it's your ignorance who's the fire starter.

Remember the one way to handle ignorance? Get understanding. With understanding, fewer relationships would collapse under the strain of miscommunication, because ignorance breeds doubt and worry.

Speakers who don't feel heard doubt their own importance and worry about what the other person thinks about them. This sets up a fear vibration the next time the speaker is in the presence of the other person. The relationship is usually suppressed and declines.

So, before you start blaming everyone in the outside world for being all awkward in their ways, let's stick to the message in this book and look to your inside world for the solution.

I'm not going to dress it up for you: true communication is the response you get. Meaning, if you tell or show someone how to do something and they end up doing it wrong, your communication wasn't clear enough. Of course, this isn't always true, but it's the right attitude to adopt and doing so keeps you on the road of never-ending personal enhancement.

### What's your learning style?

So let's get into this. First, I'm going to talk about a learning style that was designed by Walter Burke Barbe and later developed by Neil Flemming.[21] The style divides people into three categories of learning: visual, audible and kinaesthetic. The learning style is called VAK.

Without meaning to sound like I'm telling you how to suck eggs, the VAK system is the way you take in and relay information through your sense of visual (sight), audible (sound) and kinaesthetic (touch and feeling) senses. To give you an example, let's look at the same story of a car crash explained by three people, each with a different modality.

---

[21] Engage and Engage (2023) VAK learning styles: what are they and what do they mean? Engage Education |. https://engage-education.com/aus/blog/vak-learning-styles-what-are-they-and-what-do-they-mean-engage-education/.

### The visual person

I had just walked out of the front door of my house and the sun was shining in my eyes. All of a sudden, this red car whizzed by and crashed into the wall. You should have seen the size of the skid mark. The car spun around. The lights were all smashed up, every panel of the car was scratched and the dent in the bonnet was huge.

### The audible person

I had just walked out of the front door of my house; it was all quiet apart from the birds singing. All of a sudden, I heard this roar of a car engine and it made the loudest crash as it bashed into the wall. You should have heard the screech from the tires. My ear drums nearly burst. The lights exploded and pieces of the car crashed to the ground.

### The kinaesthetic person

I had just walked out of the front door; all was calm but I felt something was off. All of a sudden, my heart stopped as this car clattered into the wall and shook me to my core. I felt so bad for the driver. It must have been terrifying to skid into a wall and heartbreaking to smash your car up. I was so gutted, and I was on edge for the rest of the day. You'd feel awful if it happened to you, right?

Can you see how the same story can be explained in completely different ways, just from the way we use our physical senses to absorb and explain the events of the outside world? Can you guess which of these is my modality?

As soon as you realise that there are three different learning styles, it's easy to see where traditional educational models fall down. They're set up in large part to suit the visual student. **Watch** how I do it. **Read** the sentence again. **Look** at the formula. **Imagine** this scenario. I've **shown** you twice already. **See** how it works.

All of the above is communication and guidance that aids a visual person, but is not helpful to an audible or a kinaesthetic person. I doubt many people know this, but it does explain why a couple of kinaesthetic people from my school ended up with low grades and were labelled as having ADHD, and yet now they have successful careers working in an industry with their hands.

Kinaesthetic people learn by doing. If you need to tell them something important, take them for a walk and talk, and buy them a coffee. They'll lose focus being sat down in a soulless room watching a PowerPoint presentation.

Audible people need to hear it rather than be shown it. Don't point at a board and expect them to concentrate. Instead, tell them a story and paint pictures with your words.

Learning VAK will improve your relationships at home, at work and with your friends, because it won't take you long to work out which people in your life fall under which modality of learning.

However, it all starts with who you are. First, you need to know your own modality before you can start spotting other people's.

So, are you visual, audible or kinaesthetic?

If you're not sure, take a moment to think about the last time you truly learned something and how that was presented to you. Or think of a time when information was thrown your way and you struggled to pick up the details or forgot it instantly. How was that information shared with you? The point is: you can figure out your modality either through a process of elimination or by thinking carefully about how you learn best.

I'll give you a hint though – if you're reading this book, chances are you're a visual learner; whereas if you're listening to this as an audiobook, you're more than likely an audible learner. If you're a kinaesthetic learner, you'll be looking for opportunities to try out what you've read or heard for yourself. For me, it was glaringly obvious – and not just because my wife continues to tell me that I don't listen to her – because I've always had trouble remembering names or getting the vital details from a conversation.

## Chapter 7: You Are Insensitive

When I was working in removals, my stomach would turn into knots the moment a customer would explain over the phone or in person exactly where their house was. They thought telling me verbally was the clearest way to explain and I thought it was annoying, unhelpful and confusing. I'd ask them to send me the full address by email or text message, and they thought this was unhelpful, believing it would be easier to tell me now, while we were speaking.

I'd be getting impatient; they'd be getting impatient.

We'd be jousting because I wanted the details in writing so I could find the road by looking at a map, and find their home by looking out for their house name. I reasoned with my ignorance by thinking customers were hell-bent on making life awkward – that the "customer is always king" thing had gone to their head. My attitude towards people has improved since.

All that was happening here is that the customer was audible and I'm visual when I'm in a focused state. In fact, each modality induces each of us to fall into one of three states: focused, processing and spaced out.

Without realising, by asking for the information to be written down, all I was doing was safeguarding the information because my spaced-out state is audible. Therefore, I wanted to transfer the information into a visual format so I could use my focused visual senses to internalise it, while not being aware this could also be making the customer's life hard.

With my own VAK, I've noticed that I have a focused, processing and spaced-out state.

**Focused** – Visual
**Processing** – Kinaesthetic
**Spaced out** – Audible

Knowing how habits are formed, I'm guessing this was induced by working in removals for 21 years. The customer would show us everything they wanted moving (visual), we'd start packing the items into boxes and loading the vehicle (kinaesthetic), and then we'd communicate as we were working (audible).

When it comes to managing people at work, imagine trying to get an audible person to read the details of the assignment. That's the worst thing you can do as a manager and unfair to the employee.

This is also fun with friends. Before I learned about VAK, my audible friend would annoy the hell out of me by taking ages to reply to my text messages. I'd be thinking, "He's useless, disrespectful and can't be much of a friend if he keeps ignoring me. Our friendship can't be that important to him. The tophat."

Once I gained understanding in this area of VAK, I found out that my friend's an audible person. So I've stopped texting him. I send him voice notes and he replies right away. I always chuckle to myself now. He doesn't know he's audible, but because I do, I can improve my friendship with him by communicating in his modality. I don't know why I find it hilarious, but it is for me.

But in all seriousness, it's a gift to form those deeper connections with those who are important to you, like your husband, wife, children, friends and colleagues, just by working on yourself.

A kinaesthetic person is all about feeling, so if you tell them how you feel and how doing whatever it is you want to do is going to help with feeling better, you'll get a good response.

So that's the gist of VAK, and now I'm going to introduce you to a personality assessment that works in unison with VAK, which is called DISC. The DISC model of behaviour was first proposed in 1928 by William Mouton Marston in his book *Emotions of Normal People*.[22]

---

[22] Marston, W.M. (1928) *Emotions of Normal People*. Harcourt Brace & Company. Available at: https://doi.org/10.1037/13390-000.

Chapter 7: You Are Insensitive

### From communication to personality

VAK is a communication assessment and DISC is a personality assessment, so let's get into DISC.

First of all, there are four different ways we separate people. This is not 100 per cent definitive by the way, but you can put people into these categories. The four categories are:

- **D** which stands for dominance.
- **I** which stands for influence.
- **S** which stands for steadiness.
- **C** which stands for conscientious.

We can split these further in that the Ds and Cs are more task focused, while the Is and Ss are more people focused. In short, the Ds and Cs will prioritise the task even if it means upsetting the people they're working with. This is unlike the Is and Ss who will prioritise their relationship with the people over getting the task done. To go one step further, the Ds and Is are the outgoing personalities, whereas the Cs and Ss are more reserved.

Let's go through them one by one and see if you can spot your category.

### D = dominance

Now, the D stands for dominance because these people always want to be number one. They want to be in control. They are extremely determined and will stop at nothing to succeed and get the desired result. They're known for being outgoing, very blunt and are often misunderstood as being heartless due to their driven nature to get the task done to the best it can be.

While Ds are great leaders and certainly people you want on your side to take to war with you, they do have a tendency to put themselves out of their depth. They have ideas galore and will start loads of things and finish none of them. They need to work on their people skills in order to galvanise a team. They must touch the hearts of their troops. They don't like too many details. They focus on hard results. They're very black and white.

You'll hear Ds saying things like, "Don't give me details, get me results," "I don't care how you do it, just get it done," and "Don't tell me how you're going to do it, call me when you're done." Straight-laced people are the Ds who are just as strict with themselves. It's never meant to be personal.

### C = conscientious

The C stands for conscientious because just like the Ds, they are task oriented and will also sacrifice their relationship with the people around them to get the task done. They're task-first people who are known for being more reserved than the Ds. They talk with precision and often won't say anything unless there's meaning behind it. They're always thinking and are also misunderstood as being shy due to their will to get the task done to the best they can.

Cs can be great leaders but prefer to be led so they can master their role. This makes them more of a specialist, whereas the D is more of a generalist. The Cs would rather not be spinning loads of plates because they want to complete the task at hand to the best of their ability before moving on. Unlike the D, the C loves details. In fact, you cannot give the C too many details. It's impossible. Ds and Cs work really well together because their strengths make up for each other's weaknesses. However, an organisation with just Cs and Ds is intense. It's all work and no play.

### I = influence

The I stands for influence and unlike the Ds and Cs, people who are Is want to be liked by everyone. They prioritise people over tasks and want to make sure everyone is having a good time. They like to indulge in chit-chat and want to make sure they're putting a smile on everyone's face.

The I is enthusiastic. They like to seek approval and be popular even if it means neglecting the task, which is something D and C cannot do.

## S = steadiness

The S stands for steadiness. These people are excellent at doing the everyday repetitive work of a business because they love routine. They don't like change. Like the Cs, they are more reserved, but like the Is they are more people focused then task focused.

It's important to keep in mind that we're all a blend of the four personality types. It's just that we all have one that is most prominent, and another that tends to rear its head when there's added pressure or confusion.

When I'm in free flow, I'm predominately a visual D. This makes me an unstoppable task-oriented beast who beats down any challenge that comes my way in the most productive way with the least amount of details possible.

When I take on a task that makes me feel a little out of sorts, confused or not so sure of myself, I slip into C mode. I become withdrawn. I go heavy into gathering the details to make myself extra busy and to give me the excuse of not taking the action that makes a difference. Basically, I'm procrastinating in plain sight.

Here's an overview of how to spot each of the DISC personality types:

- **D** Likes to be number one. The visionary. Comes up with initial ideas. The starter. Likes new stuff.
- **I** Likes having lots of friends. Photos of friends and family on their desk. Life of the party. Brings people together.
- **S** Stays the same way. Loves routine. Reliable. Always there.
- **C** Details 97 pages of information they've read. If there are ten questions to ask, they'll ask 11.

### Who The Hell Are You?

**At work**
- D  You do this. You do that. Let's get this moving.
- I  Let's all come in and go for a drink after.
- S  Slowly, slowly. Slow and steady wins the race.
- C  27 steps, checklist, survey, questionnaires.

**Buying**
- D  Wants the price and makes an instant decision.
- I  Buys from the salesperson who becomes their friend.
- S  Buys from the person they dealt with last time, wants a guarantee.
- C  14 days of online research, already gone through the spec sheet, has a few last questions.

**Texting**
- D  One liners. Straight to the point.
- I  How are you? Do much at the weekend?
- S  Very simple message. Not as excitable.
- C  Long messages. Lots of words. Explaining the same thing in three different ways.

**Recognised**
- D  Others see them as a bully, obnoxious and loud.
- I  Everyone's best friend, life and soul of the party.
- S  More in the background. Sits in the corner where it's safe and calm.
- C  Reserved and are either perceived as fascinating or boring because of the details they put into conversations.

**Learning to swim**
- D  By diving in.
- I  By getting a bunch of friends to do the lessons together then having a cocktail after.
- S  By taking a lot of lessons. Improves slowly but surely.

Chapter 7: You Are Insensitive

C  By reading four to five books, watching five or six videos, reading up on the trainer's history and reading 11 online reviews before signing up for lessons.

### Better communication = win-win

The benefit of learning DISC and VAK is that they help you become a better communicator. In order to get what you want, you'll have to get good at giving people what they want, so being able to communicate at a higher level than you're currently doing is massive.

I'm sure there are many tools out there which improve your communication with others. I just find the combination of DISC and VAK a very straightforward system to use once you've learned it.

You can't help but notice when someone is outgoing and you can't stop your mind considering, "is this person a D or C?" And then you notice them say something blunt that carries the possibility of offence, and your mind goes, "Oh, they're definitely a D, because an I would never risk offending another person."

You see, you don't send a text message about a task to an audible I and expect to get the response you wanted. Given their VAK and DISC profile, the best way to communicate with them is either face-to-face or by telephone call.

The best way to communicate with a visual D is by a very short email or text message stating the result you want. Make it sound like a challenge because challenge excites them, but don't give them too many details because it drives them nuts.

With a visual C you want to communicate by email or text message and share the result you want. Tell them why you want to achieve the result, how it will help and what the thought process behind the idea is. You cannot give them enough details.

A question to ask yourself is, "Do these people want me to shake their hand with eye contact, give them a fist pump or give them a hug?"

Once you know what's happening and can understand the other

person's responses to your communication based on their VAK and DISC profiles, you'll have a revelation. All of a sudden, what used to annoy you won't bother you in the slightest. You'll see the other person for who they really are – and recognise their massive strengths, regardless of which profile and learning modality they lean towards.

I annoy my wife. She tells me I don't listen. I say no and attempt to use my "get out of jail free" card by explaining how I'm a visual D, so she should send me a text message. This has never gone down well for two reasons:

1 She shouldn't have to.
2 She's a kinaesthetic I.

Therefore, she expects me to feel her words. Communication has been good fun in our house over the years, I can tell you.

My point is that what you want in life is going to come to you through the hands of other people, and they're going to expect an equivalent in return. Being able to communicate better means you can manage and develop relationships to a win-win status.

Multi-business owner and business coach Brad Sugars takes this to a whole new level to create a winning environment for his teams. He has developed a recruitment and training system in all of his businesses that includes a DISC and VAK assessment during the interview stages to ensure he gets the right team member employed for the right position. Once this person is employed, they have a little sign on their desk that says, "I'm a visual D," (or whatever their modalities are) to remind the person who wants to talk to them how best to go about it.

Personally, I feel this is a win-win scenario and takes each person into careful consideration, which in turn makes people feel needed, important and cared for. From my experience, a person will give their heart and soul to the people and organisations who fulfil this need that all of us humans have.

The goal is to develop a good attitude towards people and treat every person you come in contact with as the most important person in the world. For as far as he or she is concerned, they are. Even though you'll never get anyone to admit it, it's true.

I have introduced you to DISC and VAK to help you understand yourself and others more thoroughly so you can communicate with and treat them better than you are currently. I hope this knowledge will also make you more adaptable, deepen your connections and help you make yourself more charming and magnetic.

**INSENSITIVE SUCCESS HABIT/** Learn what type of communicator you are in different situations and use the VAK and DISC methods I've shared here to start identifying how the important people in your life prefer to communicate. Become aware of how you could adapt your own communication style to better match theirs and see how this affects your interactions. When you get used to doing this with the people you're closest to, you'll find you start applying this to everyone you meet once you've got your head around the concepts.

I must emphasise that I'm of the opinion that there is a point where you can go too far with this technique and you can end up using it negatively to benefit yourself to the disadvantage of others. This is not what it's about.

You'll hear some sales people say you've got to match and mirror people to build rapport and lead them into the sale, almost as if you're pulling a blindfolded horse by the halter. I kind of feel it's snidey and manipulative.

Getting in touch with your senses can only be a good thing, because then you can start using them to the benefit of yourself and those you come in contact with. We're so familiar with our senses that we tend to take them for granted, and we only recognise we have them when they're gone. For example, how much do you value your sense of taste when you've got a cold? But your senses can do more than give you an appreciation of your experiences in the physical world.

### Visualise with the physical senses in mind

In your mind though, you always have your senses – you can't lose them in that imaginary world you're creating using your higher faculties. What's more, it's essential to include your physical senses in the scene you create when you're holding your ideal on the screen of your mind. If it's a new car you want, what does the steering wheel feel like in your hands? How does the seat feel against your back? How do you feel driving it? What colour is the dashboard? What pattern do the seats have? What does the engine sound like? How easy to follow are the parking sensors? What does the interior smell like? What can you taste as you're driving it? Maybe you chew gum when you drive?

Getting the five senses involved with your creative faculty work will accelerate the process of bringing it into physical form. Your subconscious mind craves sense impressions and the way you make sweet love with your subconscious mind is through giving it what it needs.

As we discussed in Chapter 4 where we learned about the subconscious, this is done either inductively or deductively, but we know the subconscious is only deductive. In other words, you program yourself by choice or by chance. There's a space between everything that happens where you have the choice to accept or reject it. Living by chance swipes this space and leaves you totally deductive. By learning about your VAK and DISC modalities, and by paying attention to other people's VAK and DISC modalities, you are living more by choice than by chance. You are taking control of building the life you want to live.

I know that sometimes this can feel hard. It can feel like it's a lot of effort to pay attention to both your VAK and DISC modalities, as well as those of the people you're interacting with. I get it.

But it's time to flip your perspective. They say that knowledge is power, so now you have this knowledge, you have the power to use it to change

## Chapter 7: You Are Insensitive

your life! I'm not saying it will all be plain sailing or that it will be easy. You are on a journey and there will be challenges ahead.

Despite how you feel about this present moment, have no doubt that...

# YOU ARE BLESSED

When my wife was diagnosed with breast cancer at 34 years old, you could forgive her for initially feeling like she was cursed on the health front. But having come through her treatment and been declared cancer-free less than two years later, she now sees the ordeal as a blessing in disguise. A warped blessing in disguise that turned up uninvited and stirred up a whirlwind of unwanted tears, terror and heartache, but a blessing nonetheless.

Not only did her initial diagnosis give us both a stark reminder that our time on this planet is temporary, it also beamed bright lights on to all of the great things we already had in our lives that we took for granted. Looking back, it was almost like a signal to stop focusing on what we were lacking in our lives, and start being grateful for everything we did have. It was like a resounding verdict from a judge's gavel that we were attaching happiness to all of the things we didn't have, and in doing so we were indirectly being ungrateful for the things that we did have.

Following the bad news, the way we viewed happiness and fulfilment changed in an instant. We changed the way we saw our children, our home, our profession and many other things that ranged from being thankful for having a tumble dryer that dried our clothes to the trees in our garden for keeping our oxygen clean. Our entire outlook on life changed and our attention shifted on to the things that really mattered.

There's nothing like staring down the barrel of eight rounds of chemotherapy treatment to put things into perspective. To change what had become an everyday sense of entitlement, when walking down the street, hearing the birds singing or drinking an instant coffee, into a privilege.

Being creatures of habit, people seldom change unless they experience a break-up, a break apart, or a breakdown. It seems to take a situation that's extreme enough to get us to review what we're doing, why we're doing it and whether it's the best possible way to do it. It's kind of funny because when something breaks, it opens. In this case, the breaking news opened up a new perspective on life.

Change was instant. One day my wife's a self-conscious person who's holding back on wearing a dress that exposes her legs, the next she's ready to lay all of her inhibitions bare to keep hold of her blonde hair.

My wife developed a new-found love for her hair the moment the doctors said that losing her hair was inevitable. My wife's awareness was expanding and her connection to her innate power was deepening, yet the doctors were talking to her about wigs. Already talking about treating a potential *effect* as if it were a foregone conclusion.

She wasn't willing to accept the doctor's vision, and I wasn't prepared to see the sad powerless look in her eye if it did happen. What could I do? Oh, since the medics are talking about effects, let's consult the Law of Cause and Effect.

**The question that sprung to mind was, "How can she treat the *cause* of hair loss?"**
The Law of Polarity states that everything has an opposite, which meant that my wife's hair could only fall out if it had the potential to stay in. One extreme couldn't possibly exist without the other. And since nothing is either negative or positive until our thinking causes it to be so, my wife made an internal decision to focus on the positive side of the polarity. The one that read, "hair stays in".

As I write this I'm aware that when my wife was going through treatment, we had not heard of *Law of Attraction* author and speaker Esther

Hicks, who says, "What you focus on grows."[23] But it's a rather fitting statement given that she was focusing on hair growth when the medics were talking about hair loss.

Anyway, I'd heard that the way someone gets sick is when their body is in a "dis-eased" state that's not at ease, which is why we use the word "disease" to describe an illness. And that a body left in a dis-eased state leads to disintegration and causes organs and senses to shut down and hair to fall out. All of these things that I'd read and not paid much attention to were all now making perfect sense.

I thought to myself, if this were true, surely then, hair couldn't fall out of a body that's at ease?

**Next question: "How can my wife put herself in 'at ease' vibration?"**
The Law of Vibration states that a person in a high vibration feels so good because the body is at ease. Albert Einstein also said that by matching the frequency of the reality you want, you cannot help but get that reality.

**"How can she raise her vibration?"**
Gratitude is the fastest way to raise your vibration.

According to the medical professionals, the odds were so stacked against my wife's wishes to keep hold of her hair that it was as if she needed some magic. The first thing that sprung to mind was a book called *The Magic* that's written by Rhonda Byrne.[24]

Rhonda Byrne is an Australian television writer and producer who's best known through her movie and book *The Secret*[25], which explains how the Law of Attraction works, and how all of the great men and

---

[23] *Esther Hicks Quote: "What you focus on grows."* (no date). https://quotefancy.com/quote/1510829/Esther-Hicks-What-you-focus-on-grows.

[24] Byrne, R. (2012). *The Magic*. Simon and Schuster.

[25] Byrne, R. (2011) The secret. Simon and Schuster.

women throughout history used the Law of Attraction to create good in their lives.

Now, I think it's not an unfair thing to say that *The Secret* helped around as many people as it confused. Through no fault of the movie, a lot of people started to believe that all they needed to do was think about what they wanted for a short while and they'd attract it. Which is not true because the Law of Attraction states that you can only attract that which is in harmony with you.

Therefore, your dominating thoughts must be on the thing you want. You simply can't be rich if the majority of the time you're thinking poor. You can't hold on to faith if you're thinking about what could go wrong. In my wife's case, she had no chance of keeping her hair if she accepted the doctor's opinion as true.

At the end of the day – and backed up by highly recommended books on how the mind works such as *Think and Grow Rich!*, *As a Man Thinketh*, and *He Can Who Thinks He Can!* – it's not someone else's mind that creates the fact, it's your mind. So, when someone's giving you advice, the only decision you need to make is whose opinion you are going to side with. Your own opinion, or someone else's?

Rhonda Byrne's book, *The Magic*, is about gratitude. It's full of simple practical action steps that anyone can do on a daily basis. The purpose of the book is to deepen your feeling of gratitude for the everyday things that are always there for you so that you feel safe, secure and even rich – regardless of what your bank balance reports.

I knew that the practices worked because magical things had happened to me when I was taking half-hearted action on the steps when I read the book a few months earlier. I noticed the energy moving through my body and I felt happier and lighter. What actually happened was that the gratitude practices put me in a positive vibration. I wasn't aware that gratitude is the fastest way to raise your vibration. But I was aware that the things I wanted were coming to me with minimum effort.

Rhonda Byrne says in the book that whatever you're grateful for, you'll attract more of. It seemed to work for me when I tried it out. Maybe it would work for my wife's hair? Anything was worth a shot, right? Even if the contents of the book did prove to be a load of gibberish, what was there to lose? I'd never heard of gratitude practices doing more harm than good.

So I bought *The Magic* book for my wife.

From the moment she started to read it, she instantly felt better in herself and the spring in her step was back for all to see. Not only did she read through the magical real-life stories, she also moved into action by following the exact gratitude practices laid out in the book.

**The first thing she did was a magical practice that Rhonda Byrne calls "Count your blessings":**

1 You write down ten things that you're grateful for.

2 Read them back and say the words "thank you, thank you, thank you" for each thing that you wrote down.

This is not to be treated as purely an intellectual exercise. You need to be truly grateful for the things you write down.

*I'm so grateful for my hair because I can style it in different ways to suit.*
*I'm so thankful for my hair because…*
*I'm so blessed to have my hair because…*

The "*because*" part is what makes you feel the gratitude deeper because you've personalised it. It's essential to express why you're grateful because you're emitting a stronger flow of energy to the thing. This gets you feeling good and thinking positive. You're looking for the good, which is a great habit to form. Just imagine how you would feel if you were in the habit of always finding the good in every situation. You'd feel good all of the time.

You'd strut through life in a state of optimism and handle whatever life throws at you. You'd know that every unfavourable circumstance holds an element that can be turned to advantage. How do we know this? Because thanks to the Law of Polarity, everything has an opposite.

My wife applied all of the gratitude practices that Rhonda Byrne laid out in the book, giving special thanks for her hair. Katie never lost her hair. Sure, more strands than usual came out between rounds of treatment, but she never lost faith and never had to wear a wig because the amount of hair that did come out was not noticeable to other people.

No one had a clue and, would you believe, that after the rounds were finished, her hairdresser reported hair regrowth straight away. Was this down to following Rhonda Byrne's suggestions? We certainly believe so. On that note, we are truly blessed to have *The Magic* by Rhonda Byrne in our lives because she kept my wife in truly great spirits throughout her two-year battle – she came out on top, by the way.

### You're richer than you realise

Dr Albert Schweitzer was a famous German doctor who won the Nobel Peace Prize for his work in medicine in 1952. He was once asked, "What's the biggest problem with the world today?" and he answered by saying, "Men simply don't think."[26] Never a truer word said and it's probably even more relevant today than when it was said back in 1952. Back then, the world was a far less information-driven environment. In today's world, ideas are thrown in your face at every turn, leaving you vulnerable to being impressed upon.

You could have this. You could have that. You should learn this. You know this. You have to watch this. Find out this one hack. Discover this one secret.

It's all about what you could or you should have; or more accurately put, what you don't have. This is why, I believe, so many people are chasing away their lives trying to outrun their self-consciousness.

---

[26] Miracle Malini (2023b) *The Strangest Secret by Earl Nightingale.* https://www.youtube.com/watch?v=l1gXZu1i8TM.

## Chapter 8: You Are Blessed

The truth is, you may be short of money and material things, but you're already rich. In contrast to the way the world profits from telling people what they haven't got, it pays dividends to spend a few minutes everyday focusing on what you have got. Because what you focus on grows.

That's right. You've got so much going for you.

If you don't believe me, just take a look at all of the things that surround you at home. You don't need most of these things. You have them because you wanted them, and those wants moved into physical form from an idea. Granted, the idea to have wooden flooring may have come to you through a photograph or a TV show, but it still started as an idea.

The fact you have all of these things is a blessing in itself because you wanted them. What often happens is that we take everything that surrounds us for granted. We're all guilty of complaining about what we don't have and not giving enough thanks for the things we do have.

To adopt a mindset that you're rich with or without material possessions is a truly blissful way to live. If you've got your health, you're rich. If you've got family and friends, you're rich. Even if you're lacking money, you're still rich. If you've got a roof over your head and warm sheets on your bed, you're rich.

You may think to yourself, "I don't like this house I live in. It's too small, there's not enough room." Well, that may be so, but what you focus on grows. So you may not like the house, but what you won't like even more than that is your subconscious accepting that idea and bringing more of it to you. It's a self-fulfilling prophecy, leaving you feeling deeper in your unideal living situation than ever before.

In order for that not to happen, all you need is a simple, yet not easy, mental adjustment. You're knee-deep through this book now so you know that all of your highs and lows stem from your mind, from the thought energy you're sending out to the world.

### Get into a gratitude habit

The most powerful way to get a positive mental adjustment is through gratitude, as I've already explained. When you take some time to give your attention to the things you already have in your life the feeling you get is incredible. Gratitude puts you in a wonderful vibration. It really does. It sends shockwaves through your fingertips and lifts you to a higher altitude of consciousness. You become more aware of the world at large rather than your own little hut of troubles. You become more patient, more calm and more happy about life. Gratitude is win-win-win.

Above all, it is so easy to do – if you do it that is – and given all the benefits that come to you, why would you not want to do it?.

When you think about habits, setting up a habit of gratitude is an absolute must. It puts you in a great vibration and lifts your vibration to a higher frequency so you can attract good things. As energy is always flowing to you, gratitude is the attitude that hooks you up to the energy supply that you want.

Ever noticed that when you're feeling good about life, everything just flows? What if there was a way for you to feel good about life and be in flow more often? There is, and gratitude is the key.

**EXERCISE: THE HABIT OF GRATITUDE/** The way to set up a habit of gratitude is to wake up every morning and write down ten things you're grateful for, and be truly grateful for them. Don't just treat this as an intellectual exercise, be truly grateful.

For example:

1. I am truly grateful for my legs and feet because they give me the freedom to roam as I please.
2. I am so blessed to have my home because it's such a lovely safe haven for me and my family.

## Chapter 8: You Are Blessed

3   I give thanks to running water and the access I have to it because I can use it to drink, bathe in, clean things, nourish the garden, regulate my car engine, make ice and squirt my children from the hosepipe in the summer.

Once you've written ten things, read over each one either in your mind or out loud, and then say the magic words, *thank you, thank you, thank you*. If you are truly grateful for these things, you will feel an instant change in the way you feel.

All of your worries and niggles will evaporate because you're plugged into a frequency of graciousness, goodness and abundance. You'll feel like you're already brimming with good things in your life, and anything else that comes your way will be an added bonus.

Guess what? More good things will come to you, multiplied by being on the same frequency. You'll be vibrating on the path of least resistance. It's the very opposite to the saying of "what you resist, persists".

Most people need a strong cup of coffee to get them going in the morning. They're grasping on to an outside solution when the best medicine comes from within. Setting up an attitude of gratitude as soon as you wake up has you fired up and chomping at the bit before you've even had your breakfast. It's the perfect antidote to chaos.

I'm not saying don't have a coffee. I'm saying have a coffee and enjoy it. Don't lose the joy of drinking a morning coffee by using it as a substance to get you going – you'll end up with the shakes. Instead, you can wind up all the go you need from within through the use of morning gratitude.

Then you can embark upon your day piped up to your own energy supply. Again, this habit is a way to control your state of vibration and the flow of energy that's attracted to you in the outside world.

You don't have to only practise gratitude in the mornings, you can practise it throughout the day as much as you like. I just believe that every person should set up a habit of gratitude last thing at night before they go to sleep, and first thing in the morning. The reason to do it last thing at night is so you wake up in a good mood. The reason to do it in the morning is so you start off your day in a good mood.

You'll notice little problems just bounce off you when you're piped up to gratitude. Bad things just cannot stick to someone who's in a good vibration.

The morning is a good time for me due to the heightened focus I find I have then. Maybe the night is better for you – that's for you to decide. You learn by doing, so it's only by doing the gratitude practices that you will find out where it's most effective for you. Experiment.

I subscribe to the idea that happiness is the best medicine, and once you experience the joy that gratitude brings to you, I'm sure happiness will have recruited another member.

All you have to do is devote around 20 minutes of your 24-hour day to sending thanks to the everyday stuff that's always there for you, to give a little grace and acknowledgement to all of the easily unnoticed special things you have in your life.

I can give you another example of the power of gratitude having also worked from following the steps laid out in *The Magic*:

**EXERCISE: HAVE A MAGICAL DAY/** There's a practice in *The Magic* called a magical morning.[27] This is when you give thanks to the things that are going to happen in the day as you're getting dressed in the morning. You do this in your mind by saying things like, "Thank you for the meeting with Steve. Thank you for the great outcome of the day. Thank you for the client who made me laugh out loud." At the end of the practice, you say, "And thank you for the magical news I received today."

Try it, I dare you.

That last sentence is crazy. The first day I did this, the news I received came from within. It was the exact event in my life that was the cause of my social anxiety and the pattern I continued running into adulthood.

---

[27] Byrne, R. (2012) *The Magic*. Simon and Schuster, page 111.

As I explained in Chapter 6, knowing the root cause of your limiting beliefs allows you to actually deal with them. Understanding this was a gamechanger for me.

The amount of fantastic news that has come to me ever since is nuts. I do this every morning and it staggers the mind.

### Take nothing for granted

It's amazing what's taken for granted. The everyday things that we just expect to be there, as though they're waiting around for us to use them, even though we give them the shoulder day after day.

Things like the spoon and bowl that we use to eat our cereal with. Imagine how hard it would be eating your cereal without having a bowl and a spoon. This simple everyday thing you're so accustomed to that you probably don't even notice it.

In fact, rather than thank them, you probably moan at them in your mind, because once you've finished you've got to wash them up and put them back in the cupboard. It's almost as if they're an annoyance. Instead of focusing on how they play a small yet integral part in your life, you send more negative energy to them through the thought of the household chores.

What about your shoes? When was the last time you thanked them? Just think about how uncomfortable it would be walking to work without shoes. How sore would your feet be? Not having shoes would certainly slow down your life. How many great things would not happen in the world without the builders wearing safety boots. There would be no venues for starters.

You may have a glass of water when you wake up to replace the fluids lost when you were asleep. You have a guaranteed supply of cold or hot water at your beck and call, and with the twist of a tap, you have an instant flow of water that's safe to drink and keeps your body hydrated.

So many people say they don't have enough money. Every time they say that, they're being ungrateful for the money they have, and therefore more money is not going to be attracted to them. To get more money you have to be immensely grateful for the money you do have. All of the bills your money is paying for allow you to have a roof over your head, give you instant access to water and pay for the groceries every week.

That's another thing: most people moan about the price of the grocery shop, when in the grand scheme of things, when you look individually at the things that are in the shopping bags, you're buying all of these items at rock-bottom prices.

All of the items you buy each week are coming from all corners of the world at a cost of billions in machinery, haulage, employment and shipping, and they end up on a shelf for you to buy at a minimal cost to feed your family. You can buy all of the cleaning products to clean your clothes, bed sheets, dishes and towels for the price of a steak meal.

You have the internet streamed right into your home so you can play games, build a business, create, connect with others or get the answer to your question in a fraction of a second. No thanks is given to it. All I hear is, "The internet is slow. The wifi won't connect. Technology stresses me out." Imagine life as we know it without the internet. You also probably have 24-hour-a day TV entertainment in your living room with hundreds of channels so you can pick and choose what you want to watch, but you're probably still guilty of saying that there is nothing to watch.

It's safe to say that where there is lack in your life, there's lack of gratitude. Say you lack money – that's the first place to start showing gratitude so you can attract more of it. Money is a servant at the end of the day, not your master. Therefore, like a servant, it is helping you move through life, so the least you can do is say thanks.

The amazing thing is that when you start giving thanks for what you believe you lack, you will start to see that lack turn into abundance.

### Use gratitude to increase your vibration

Which brings me to another point. It's a crying shame how many people are throwing away their "thank yous". Never again say thank you without really meaning it and feeling it in your body. The rewards will pay you dividends, I can assure you. Don't just say, "thank you" like it's the polite and right thing to do in this politically correct society of ours. Rather than saying "thank you" like an emotionless robot, say the words "thank you" with feeling, or don't say them all.

At the end of the day, we're all meddling our way through life and another person should be made to feel valued by receiving the next person's grace. Just think of the warm feeling you leave them with when you send thanks to someone who's helped you in some way. You, of course, know how nice it feels when you're receiving someone's gratitude.

Not only that, but when you say thank you and really mean it, you will feel incredible too. Gratitude delivers instant gratification. As soon as you give, you get back an immense feeling of love and warmth inside.

It's so powerful, it even works when you're having trouble with a past or present relationship. This is going to sound like it's coming from left field, but don't turn your nose up at my suggestion until you try it.

When someone is bothering you, go somewhere quiet and write down ten things you're grateful for about them. At first this may feel hard, but stick with it because it works wonders in either transforming a present relationship or by giving inner peace to a past relationship.

You may resist doing this because the other person has upset you or caused you some pain, but it's not about them. It is about you being in a good mood. Through using this method, you can get yourself on a higher frequency than the troublesome event and make it feel more or less obsolete.

It is just like thinking negatively or positively. You can stay in a bad vibration or a good vibration, but you can't stay in both at the same time. So, since you have a choice, it makes sense to stay in a good vibration so you enjoy your days more and get on the frequency of the good. I'm sure you'd take that over staying in a bad vibration that has you banging your knee on the table, spilling your coffee and being forced to steer yourself to safety because a car cuts you off.

### Who The Hell Are You?

Always think back to the concepts of our inside and outside worlds. Other people are part of your outside world.

Since this is the part you don't have exclusive control over, you can't let someone else put you in a bad mood. When you allow this to happen, you're giving your power away to them, leaving you totally deductive. This is no way to live a life that's been solely given to you.

You can be grateful for an insane amount of things. Your shoes that keep you comfortable. Your clothes that keep you covered up and stylish. Your wardrobe so that you can keep your clothes in an orderly fashion. Your lungs that let air come in and out of your body. Your heart for pumping blood around your body even when you're asleep. Your bed sheets for keeping you warm at night. Your fan for keeping your cool at night. Your mode of transport that takes you from place to place. The mornings for being still. The evenings for being chilled. The list just goes on and on.

And yet so many people are walking around with a chip on their shoulder like nothing good ever happens to them, as if they're so deprived from the rich life they're already part of.

I'll hold my hands up for also walking around with my shoulders slumped through concentrating on the things I'm lacking. Let me tell you, it's a dumb game because, when you think about it, there's always going to be something new to chase. Something you don't have. It is good to want things, but to want everything under the sun and feel sorry for yourself for not having it all is perhaps when you start leaning into greed and petulance. You need to be mature and patient.

In fact, a lack of patience is a form of fear, especially when you just have to look around you to see that you're already rich. You have breath, clothes, water, warmth and shelter. You may not have much money left after you've paid your bills, but let's not forget that the money you do have paid for all your bills.

Care to think about how you'd feel if you couldn't pay all your bills?

As Rhonda Byrne says in *The Magic*, "Gratitude really is the magic of life."

What about all of the people who have left a positive influence on your life? You can bathe your mind in those moments and see how you've used the wisdom passed on to you positively throughout your life so far.

I think back to some of my football coaches. Some minor thing they said that didn't make sense when I was 12 but makes a whole lot of sense now – remember the story about my friend's dad telling us we couldn't be professional footballers if we couldn't play with both feet? That's one of the moments I give thanks for, because it shaped me in a positive way. The funny thing is that my friend's dad probably doesn't even remember saying it.

**BLESSED SUCCESS HABIT/** Make giving thanks and showing gratitude one of your daily activities. You can do that in any of the ways I've suggested in this chapter. All I ask is that when you're doing your gratitude practice, you pause and really *feel* it.

The lesson is that we have to give thanks to the everyday things we've all been guilty of taking for granted. With such rich resources at our fingertips like running water and toothpaste, we've become so accustomed, expectant and, dare I say it, entitled that we can end up being ungrateful through neglect. Do you grumble about the price of the weekly shop that feeds your family for a week, and yet you happily go to a restaurant and spend the same amount on one slap-up meal and think nothing of it?

That's OK, you're not perfect and neither am I, nor that person you admire.

Know that…

# YOU ARE UNDER CONSTRUC- TION

It doesn't matter how many books, online courses and seminars you've done up until this point; if you're not getting the results you want, you've not yet developed a full understanding of the information you've taken on.

That's OK because you are under construction as the person you're wishing to become. Gaining new knowledge is important for the development of new ideas, but just like positive thinking on its own, continuing to load up on knowledge is not everything.

To reiterate what I said in Chapter 1: you're already full, so you don't need filling up. You need to create, develop and draw out the magnificence that lies dormant inside of you.

You may have been to the seminar, shaken hands with the speaker and have stacks of notes, but have you just nodded in agreement with the ideas and not taken the time to think about them? Have you played with them and written a description of what you learned in your own words? I recommend you take one line of your notes and write what it means in your own words, and continue doing this.

If you've just filled up your notebook and your consciousness for the day, you've just gathered someone else's knowledge and haven't drawn any of your infinite potential out. A few days later, your full notebook sits closed in the corner of a room, your consciousness fills with what's going on around you and you've made zero progress on your investment of knowledge.

That's why knowledge in itself is nothing more than potential ideas for you to work with so you can bring more of yourself to the surface. Taking on knowledge alone may develop your memory, but I would question how much it's developed your mind and your life.

I've often thought that the benefits of knowledge are always the other side of an unlocked door that's shut, meaning you still have to walk to the door to not only open it, but then walk through and into better things. In other words, you need to ask questions, write a debrief in your own words and create an action step. Basically, you have to act. Act on the knowledge you've taken on or it's worthless to you. It was a bad investment. You should have saved the £350 you spent on the seminar and watched a free conspiracy theory on YouTube instead – only joking, but you know what I'm getting at.

I know I'm babbling on here because I don't want you to fall into the same trap I fell into. Like a rabbit caught in the headlights, I had the philosophy that I would make up for my deficits by learning like a nutter. It was a flawed plan because I misunderstood how learning is best done through repetition. I thought dwelling on something I'd just read or heard was slowing me down. I needed to get on to the next thing, because that might be where the secret lay.

When I fell into the world of personal development and my RAS kicked in, I saw books, courses, podcasts, forums and seminars everywhere. Out came the debit card and I started buying book after book, course after course and going to seminar after seminar trying to find the secret.

The only secret I found was that there was no secret. I did know that most of it, just like this book, was a regurgitation of past material. But the thing that gets confusing is that the message is said one hundred different ways, so you end up flipping from mentor to mentor not really getting anywhere.

## Chapter 9: You Are Under Construction

The reason for this is because you haven't locked into the material. You read the book once and nothing changed, so you moved on to the next book. But reading a book once through means the contents of the book couldn't have possibly been understood.

You never learned to ride your bike by trying once, and then moving on to the next bike. You learned through picking the bike back up and trying again. You did this over and over and programmed yourself to ride the bike.

I've heard struggling business people who worked with Brad Sugars, the guy who pioneered business coaching and who is considered one of the best business coaches in the world, say their business didn't improve using Brad's methods, so they moved on to a new mentor.

And yet, Brad's business formulas are not only proven in thousands of his clients' businesses, but Brad also runs nine to ten businesses of his own, buys and sells businesses for a living and uses all the formulas he teaches in his own successful businesses.[28] But you get people who try the formulas once or twice and then give up and say they don't work. The truth is, when you don't work at something, it won't work for you.

So you could spend your whole life acquiring new knowledge and skills in a quest to move you on to better things. But while they're integral parts of your personal growth journey, knowledge and skills can only get you so far.

### Plant your ideal in your subconscious mind

Have you ever wondered how less knowledgeable people than you are exceeding you in terms of success in the areas you want to succeed in?

Have you ever thought, "That person is lucky or everything seems to happen to that person. I know I have far more knowledge and have way more skills than that person, and yet they're getting the results I want to

---

[28] https://bradsugars.com/free-downloads/

get." That person is succeeding because of the ideas they have planted in their subconscious mind.

Don't be so hard on yourself. I just want to put it out there because, if you're anything like me, you're most probably a driven person who has a tendency to put far too much pressure on yourself.

I will tell you this though: you have time to plant what you want in your subconscious mind, but you must start now. Not tomorrow, not the next day, not when you get back from holiday, not from the start of the month. NOW.

When you're chasing down an ideal, you can end up always feeling so far away from the goal and fail to pay any attention to just how far you've come. I've noticed this is said a lot, but I don't feel it's emphasised enough, so people just brush over it. Let me say it again in a slightly different way: you need to look back sometimes to see how far you've come, even if you're still focusing on your ideal future. I would hear this and think, "Yeah, yeah. Easy for you to say now that you've broken through." But it's true.

One of the best ways I've found to combat this, and remind myself how far I've come, is with a self-appreciation journal. I urge you to get yourself a self-appreciation journal and write about your progress month to month so you can look back and be proud of yourself when you see how much you've grown.

> ***Example:*** *It's the end of July and I'm over the moon that I have written two chapters of my book. At the start of the month, I gave myself a command to write at least one sentence every day, and, even if it just ended up being an idea I added to the notes of my phone, I did it. While writing, I ran into a limiting belief that went, "No one wants to read what I'm writing about," so I did the work to remove the belief and replaced it with, "People love reading up on how they can improve their lives, and since I write about how people can get way more out of themselves through using what they already have, everyone will be intrigued by*

*my writing." Well done on another successful month of moving forward.*

In order to get where you are today, you've had to overcome a whole host of challenges and had to grow so much as a person. To get where you want to go requires the same. But just think, you've taken on challenge after challenge throughout your life and you've overcome it all. Every one of them. Let that sink in for a moment. You have overcome everything in your life to date. You've handled it all. You can be proud of that.

**The paradox of fear**

This brings me to fear. Fear makes no sense when you think about it, so let's try and make some sense of it. Fear is nothing more than false expectations appearing real. When you boil it down, fear is just a belief that you can't handle something. That's all it is.

The best way to overpower it is by knowing that if the worst were to happen, you'd handle it. How do you know that? Because you're still here today. You've handled everything that's been thrown your way. You survived all of the fear you've felt so far and you probably didn't even meet the majority of your fears in the flesh anyway.

It was Mark Twain who allegedly said, "Some of the worst times in my life never actually happened."

He has neatly captured that paradox of fear – that often what we fear isn't the reality we live in. We fear a particular situation or outcome, even though there is no guarantee of that negative situation or outcome arising. In fact, the opposite is often true – let's say you've spent days worrying about a meeting with your boss, feeling as though you might be reprimanded or even fired. On the day of the meeting you're so nervous you feel sick. The meeting happens, and instead of losing your job, you're told you're doing excellent work and will be in line for a pay rise at the end of the year.

How much time did you waste worrying, when you could have been doing something more productive? Not only that, but worrying was completely pointless. Even if you had been fired, would worrying about it for days beforehand have changed the outcome? I think not.

Although this sounds harsh, to be fearful is ignorance of the self. By studying fear and understanding what it is, you'll see it for what it really is. Nothing. Fear doesn't exist unless we allow it to exist.

The way to deal with everything you're having a challenge with is by snooping around in its opposite. The Law of Polarity is your friend. So much so that when you consider that the opposite of fear is faith, instantly your perception shifts. You relate faith with hope and possibilities that send positive thought waves through your body.

On the face of it, fear and faith are both believing in something that hasn't shown up yet. Since faith has been hailed as a vital ingredient towards success over and over again and fear never helps anybody without causing suffering, you're best to develop faith.

Impatience is fear. Feeling frustrated and like you're not making any progress is fear that you're not moving towards what you want. Do you know what you want? Have you set goals? If not, why not?

## Set ideals to power your progress

The human is a goal-striving machine, and so it needs a goal to give it direction. If you don't have goals of your own, it's likely that you're being directed by other people's goals, almost as if you're building someone's else's dream at the expense of your own dream.

Another word I like to use is the word "ideal" when I'm talking about goals. It helps me when I'm goal setting and giving myself direction. When I read back a new goal, I always ask myself if this is the most ideal possible outcome. Although the goal itself is a stepping stone towards a worthy ideal (as I'll explain in more detail shortly), I don't want the goal to be a stepping stone towards a less than ideal situation. I want to achieve the best possible outcome for each goal, and to do that I need to

## Chapter 9: You Are Under Construction

know exactly what the ideal looks like. So, I'm thinking backwards – or starting with the end in mind.

I've found goals can be too easily misunderstood as to-do items. It's not a goal when you know how to do something already – that's merely a task. It's usually just something you haven't done yet. A goal has to be something that you have no clue how to achieve, but you know it's what you want. You must set goals that the present model of you cannot achieve. Goals are not to get. Goals are to grow. So to keep this fresh in my mind, I find the word "ideal" helps.

Plus, Earl Nightingale, author and success expert, used the word "ideal" in his definition of success, a definition that I believe absolutely hits the nail on the head. He defined success by saying, "Success is the progressive realisation of a worthy ideal."[29] This means if you're a person who wants to write a book, and you're progressively moving towards that goal, then you're a successful person. If you're saving for a down payment on your first house, and you're progressively stacking up money, then you're a successful person.

It really doesn't matter what you want because we all want different things. Whether it be a financial ideal, a health ideal, or a relationship ideal, it's up to you to come up with the ideal. Don't forget, everything you want is already here, if not in one state, then in another.

If you've not taken yourself out of the madness of the day and sat down and thought about a worthy ideal, you won't be moving towards the realisation of something that came from within.

Based on Earl Nightingale's definition of success, an unsuccessful person is someone who doesn't have an ideal because they have nothing to progressively move towards. I wholeheartedly agree with this idea. Your results are always under construction. Even if you're only taking baby steps every day, you are still moving towards your goal and ideal life.

However, without a worthy ideal, you cannot set goals.

---

[29] Miracle Malini (2023) *The Strangest Secret by Earl Nightingale.* https://www.youtube.com/watch?v=l1gXZu1i8TM.

## How worthy ideals differ from goals

Worthy ideals are what you uncover in your imagination. Let's say you're visualising your dream home; you're never going to uncover the details of every room in a 20-minute visualisation. You're going to extract the details day after day and transfer the information on to paper in the form of writing or drawing. This takes time.

In your mind, you're going to see the colour of the carpets, the layout of your bathroom, the TVs on the walls, the fabric of your sofa, the pictures hanging on the walls of your study, your clothes in your walk-in wardrobe, your cars in your garage and so on.

Worthy ideals are the "perfect world" scenarios that you want to see play out even though you have no idea how to make them happen. A goal, on the other hand, is a stepping stone towards living your worthy ideal – such as living in your dream home.

The worthy ideal that I've imagined for this book is to sell 5,000 copies in the first year of its release. The goal to move me in that direction right now is to submit the first draft of the book. The next goal is to edit draft two. The next goal is to design the cover. The next goal is to build a marketing system. The next goal is to get the book live. Do you see where I'm going here and what I mean by worthy ideals acting as a North Star and the goals being the stepping stones?

Since our results are always under construction, so are the pictures we see in our minds. By forming the pictures in your mind by closing your eyes and giving your imagination a 20-minute workout each day, you can construct your ideal world. As I said earlier, it's already there, but by exercising your imagination you can put yourself in it and sharpen the picture.

What kind of stone is your dream home made out of? Does it have an in-and-out driveway with electronic gates? What's the colour of the tiles in the bathroom? What clothes are in your walk-in wardrobe? Do you have gardeners? Do you have an in-home cinema?

Day by day you can literally walk yourself around your dream home in your mind and its decor will reveal itself. You may think this is a

## Chapter 9: You Are Under Construction

silly idea. Immature, even. But this is how the lightbulb, the radio, the iPhone and everything around you was formed.

As I explained in Chapter 4, since your subconscious mind has no reasoning factor, and cannot tell real life from fantasy land, it will accept whatever pictures flash up as reality. What's more, as the subconscious mind doesn't sleep, it works night and day at bringing the picture into physical form.

It's giving you ideas, thoughts and suggestions all the time. If you act on them – huge IF here – you will move yourself closer to your dream home, your dream partner or whatever your ideal world is.

I use the dream home as an example because everyone has a dream home. I bet the dream home I have in my mind is different from the way yours looks in your mind. Even if we were both visualising at the same time, and were being guided by the same voice telling us to step into our master bedroom, the pictures in our minds would be totally different.

Not only that, but I guarantee that if five people were guided to picture their ideal kitchen, their driveway or their garden, all five people would have a completely different picture in their minds – the fact that the picture is different for each person doesn't matter. The point is, it's a picture they can return to any time they like by closing their eyes and imagining themselves being there. They can unveil every detail from the colour of the roof tiles to the smell of their bath and the birds singing on a sunny spring morning.

That's why this is a personal deal. When you imagine and construct a worthy ideal in your mind, you're the only one who's seen it because you're the only one who went there. Not your spouse, not your kids, not your best friend, only you. No one else can step into your mind and see the world as you see it through your creative faculties.

But everyone could stand next to you and look out at the exact same view through your physical senses. You could stand next to me on the beach and see the same rocks, the same view of the horizon, hear the plane flying overhead, feel the same breeze against your skin and smell the same sea air. We could share an outer experience.

But when it comes to our inside world, we're having totally different experiences. You might be totally relaxed because you've got a week off and I could be worked up because I'll be dealing with a problematic customer when I return to work after lunch.

That's why you must connect with your inside world. Your frustration comes from trying to blend in, but you were born to stand out. You're not here to conform to the rules of another person. You're here to create, develop and draw out from within. That takes a fair amount of understanding because we've all been trained to fall into line and follow orders, and to believe someone else's opinion is more valid than our own.

### Embrace your differences

Yet, we're all different so we should be different. Not for the sake of being different, but because we are different. No one should cause other people pain, unrest and upset just because they're different – that's missing the point. The point I'm trying to make is that you have the ability to think. The ability to accept or reject your own ideas or someone else's ideas. Therefore, conforming to the way things have always been done, just because that's the way it's always been done, does not mean that the existing way is the best way of doing things.

All innovation comes from imagination. You just can't get it out of a manual.

You're born with innovation piped up to your bloodstream, but probably you're just not using it.

I'll say it again. Creation is finished. What you want is already here. If you want a Ferrari, the Ferrari is already here in physical form because other people are driving them. If you want the dream home that's in your mind, it's already here in your mind.

You just need to get in harmony with it.

**UNDER CONSTRUCTION SUCCESS HABIT/** Spend five minutes meditating on who you want to be in your life every day. Ask yourself that question, close your eyes and sit with it in silence. It will come. What shows up in your mind is what Wallis D. Wattles, the author of *The Science of Getting Rich*, refers to as a "formless substance". So, go and write it all down to bring the idea into physical substance.

Do that every day, and every day you will get more and more details to add to your worthy ideal. Write them all down and soon enough you'll know exactly how you want to dress, how you want to walk and how you want to talk, and then you'll find yourself walking and talking like you imagined in your mind. I guarantee it will be more detailed than you can imagine now – and that you'll have become addicted to this process.

This work will turn your whole life around. Mark my words. Mark the words of all the people before me who achieved massive success by applying these principles.

Some things are permanent, and everything you read in this book is permanent. I will never be able to tell you who the hell you are. This is a personal deal. In much the same way as life is dull only to dull people, life is exciting only to exciting people and life is successful only to successful people, what you bring into life in your worthy ideal is what you will end up living in the physical realm we all inhabit. So, I ask you again, what kind of life do you want to have? One that's exciting, successful or full of love? Or one that's dull, boring and full of lack?

### Spotting the steps to success

I'd like you to take a moment to think about what it takes for you to lie down in your bed at night and say to yourself that today was a successful day. What things must you have done? Think back to the days where you felt successful and pinpoint exactly what you did.

I bet it was the little things you did that made all the difference – little things like exercise, making a decision and getting something done, or even just cleaning the windows. All these things compounded, and that made you feel centred, in control and amazing. It may have only been one small thing you did differently on the days you felt successful to the ones you didn't.

I suggest you write yourself a list of these things and make a conscious effort to do these things every day. Turn them all into habits so that you're having successful days on autopilot. You're being successful without conscious thought.

Once you get the little things down, it's human nature to start raising the bar for yourself and going after the bigger things. You're a goal-striving machine, after all, so it's inevitable to want to improve.

That's a great place to be in because what you want is already here. If not in physical form in the outside world, it's in your mind. You may say, "Well, it didn't exist before because I've just created it in my mind." However, that's not entirely true – it was already there, you merely revealed it.

The reason why you couldn't see it before is because you can only see the contents of your consciousness. If you're letting the outside world control you, then your consciousness is constantly being loaded with everything going on outside. Your mind keeps taking things in, like a dump truck. As I said in Chapter 8, just think about all the messaging you're being bombarded with every single day – and most of it centres on what you lack rather than what you have.

### Move from fantasy to reality

So, when you start using your imagination, you're not so much creating a vision as you are waking the dream. You're bringing the picture closer to you and taking in the details. This makes you more aware of what's meant to happen in your world.

You're not trapped where you are, you're just used to it. You gave up on the dreams in your imagination and made peace with where you are. You've made where you are your default setting. Your belief is that you've arrived and that it's silly to fantasise. You believe you're "down to

## Chapter 9: You Are Under Construction

earth" because you've made sense of the mundane life the majority of society has also made sense of. Logic has you by the balls. Your overriding belief is that you're not good enough, which is absolute nonsense.

When asked how Oasis became one of the most iconic bands in the world, both Gallagher brothers can be heard saying in multiple interviews, "It was pure belief." Not that they were the best musicians. Not that they wrote the best songs. It was pure belief.

What they had done was flooded their conscious minds with visions of roaring stadiums, touring the world and living life in a "mad for it" way. They played with this idea day after day through practice, conversation and storytelling, talking about things that hadn't even happened yet, like playing a show at their beloved football team's stadium, Maine Road, which they did in 1996.

But they were talking about it years before it happened. Most people at the time probably accused them of fantasising, which is exactly what they were doing. I don't think they knew they were doing it, or that they knew that all greatness comes from fantasy, but it didn't matter, they were working in harmony with the laws of vibration and attraction.

Both Liam and Noel Gallagher have rarely ever agreed on anything, but they both agree that belief is a major part of success – and that's a running theme I'm sure you've spotted within this book.

Connor McGregor, the Irish mixed martial artist, was filmed saying that when people ask him if success is 50 per cent mindset and 50 per cent physical, he tells them that success is 100 per cent mindset.[30] This is why I spent time talking about identifying both your limiting and empowering beliefs earlier in this book, so you can work on programming your mindset in such a way that it sets you up for success.

There's no middle road here. You may think you have beliefs that are neither hurting nor helping you, but let me tell you, they're on the

---

[30] *Mcgregor Forever | Netflix Official Site* (2023). https://www.netflix.com/gg/title/81231181.

verge of hurting you. So, if you skimmed over the part about your belief systems in Chapter 6, I urge you to revisit it, now!

You've got to make peace with the fact that there's no finish line to personal development. The world is always changing at a rapid rate, and if you don't change, you get left behind. As the saying goes, "Time waits for no man," and the world won't wait for you. If you stop re-evaluating who you are, you won't take any new action that promotes growth, which means the greatness, goodness and abundance you share with the world shrinks. You're either growing or shrinking. There's no inbetween. You can't stand still because the Law of Vibration states that everything moves and nothing rests. If you stand still for too long, then by default you'll end up being flung backwards by the energy that relentlessly flows to and through you.

Make it your mission in life to identify and remove anything you're holding inside that holds you back in life. Believe me when I tell you that after you've celebrated hitting your goal, you're then ready to grow into your next goal. You've never quite made it to the point where you can take your foot off the gas and live out your days with your feet up because you can always keep growing and do better. In other words, you're always under construction.

It's kind of like the school years. Year 1 is preparing for Year 2. Year 2 is preparing for Year 3, Year 3 is preparing for Year 4, and on it goes. So many people leave school, stop developing and find themselves constantly behind the curve. You don't want to do the same when you reach your goals because you'll get overtaken by life too. I look at all of the wins and challenges I run into this year as preparation for next year.

## What do you look like in your mind?

That might be the most important question you're ever going to ask yourself.

It sounds like a funny question but it's vitally important, and an essential part of how you're "constructing" yourself. Hear me out.

## Chapter 9: You Are Under Construction

The reason why this question is so important is that everyone has an internal self-image as well as an external visual image of themselves.

You know you get a visual picture of yourself when you look in the mirror. What you might not be aware of is that you have a self-image that you see in your mind's eye. You have a picture of yourself in your mind, and this picture is far more important than the one you see in the mirror.

The image in the mirror might get you an attractive partner, but the image in your mind determines whether you keep the partner, get married, have a family and live a happy life in each other's company.

So, you need to think about exactly who you will be when your wants are fulfilled. Will you be someone with a good attitude? If so, how would you meet, greet and cater for people? What clothes would you wear if money was no issue?

Who would you be if you couldn't feel fear and you knew you couldn't fail?

Let's say you're an anxious introvert but you see yourself as a calm, confident and calculated person in your mind – you can become that person. You could be a stay-at-home parent with no business skills, but if you see yourself as an online entrepreneur with an automated business, then you can become that person.

Your belief system, your habits, your understanding, your results and your self-image. All of these things are under construction, and you're the one who's in charge of building them or neglecting them.

From one success-driven person to another, you can recreate yourself into the exact person you want to become. The fact is…

# YOU ARE ONE ACT AWAY

Stella Adler was an American actress who performed in film and theatre from 1922 to 1951. She was a fierce lady who believed the job of an actor was to become the part they're playing through use of the imagination rather than through memory. In 1949, she founded The Stella Adler Studio of Acting in New York so she could teach her method of acting.

Her students included world-famous actors like Robert De Niro, Marlon Brando and Diana Ross. She taught them to embody the character they were playing and not to draw from their own past experiences.

In her opinion, amateur actors make the mistake of relying on the thoughts, feelings and actions they derive from themselves in order to represent the different characters they play. However, in doing so they limit themselves to only being able to portray that which they have experienced in real life.

When you think about it, this makes sense because if you were cast to play the King or Queen of England, you can't draw on the memory of when you were the prefect at school, the captain of a sports team or the owner of a business to help you act like the head of the monarchy. Or let's say you're cast to play the part of a mother or father who's grieving the loss of a child – you can't solely draw on the grief you felt when your pet hamster passed away if you want to succeed at playing the part of a grieving parent.

That's why Stella taught her students to use their imaginations to get to know who the person in the script actually was. She taught her students to focus on the details. What their character's upbringing was like. What their favourite food is. What habits they have. What they believe in. What clothes they wear at home. What clothes they wear in public. Why do they wear the clothes they wear? What school did they go to? And so on…

"You're not acting words," Stella would bellow to terrified students as she banged her hand on the table.

Now, I'm sure Stella Adler would shoot my explanation of her method down in flames, but I've done my best to explain it in a simple form. Once an actor knows how their character thinks and feels about things that happen in life, the actor knows exactly how their character will react to the drama presented in the script. Therefore, when it comes to playing the part, the acting is as natural as getting up in the morning and making a cup of coffee.

So, how does this help you?

Well, your life is essentially a movie that's playing out in real time, and you're the lead character.

As I said in Chapter 2, imagine living your entire life without ever assuming the leading role of your own show. In this version of your life, you cast aside all of your wants, dreams and desires and instead settled for playing the role of an extra in your own movie – except it's not a movie, this is your life. The last thing any ambitious person wants to feel as they approach the end of the road is that they sidestepped the path of potential and instead scurried down mediocre street.

The only way to be the star of your show is to act like the person you want to become. In order to do this, you need to know who that person is. What I'm saying is that you need to be the writer, actor and director of your own movie in order to live a truly fulfilling life. You need to write the script and then act the part. But where does the script come from? It can only come from one place – the mind.

So, just like Stella Adler's students, I'm suggesting you put your imagination to work and think up the version of you that you want to be. Not the half-baked version of you that you settle for everyday. Not the version of you that you think your spouse, kids, family, friends, boss, neighbours or in-laws think you should be. The version of you that is totally aligned with how you want to live.

**Have some fun with this exercise.**

**EXERCISE STAGE ONE: VISUALISE YOUR "CHARACTER"/** Pretend you're a screenwriter for a film and you're creating a character from scratch that just happens to be a modified version of you. The showroom model of you, if you like. This version of you is the complete package who's polished up to the nines. Just think: if money wasn't an issue, you knew you couldn't fail and no one had ever told you that you couldn't do something, how would you be living your life right now? That's the main character for your script.

What would this character of you look like? What would you think? What clothes would you wear? Would you tolerate small talk? How would you respond to being trapped in a lift? What would you say to someone who's screaming in your face? How would you look at problems? What does your voice sound like? What would you say to your spouse over breakfast? What would you eat for breakfast? How often would you exercise? Where would you go on holiday? What does your body look like? Are your legs toned? Do you smile much?

So, since you're going to use your imagination to define a character that's the best version of you, you need to find a quiet spot where you can sit or lie with your eyes closed, undisturbed for ten minutes. Use whatever time you can spare, but I recommend a minimum of ten minutes per day with your eyes closed to give yourself time to relax and the images to form. You cannot overdo this process. Make it a daily habit and I almost guarantee you'll fall in love with it. When you commit to doing this every day, you're going to find that, bit by bit, you will unveil the person you were born to be.

### Who The Hell Are You?

> Start by settling into your quiet spot, set a timer on your phone if you're strapped for time and close your eyes. Now, consider yourself breezing through the whirlwind of a busy day with no weight on your shoulders. The unshakeable you that's well rested, well dressed and who talks with conviction. A financially independent person who's surrounded by family and friends and appears to hold all the answers to life. The unstoppable you who's cool, calm and composed because you've figured it all out. You with the world in the palm of your hands.

The goal of this exercise is to end up with a crystal-clear image of the person you want to become. The more specific you are, the faster you will move the new image you hold of yourself into physical form. The side benefit of defining an image of the person you want to become in your mind is that you will also improve your present self-image by default. This is a major plus because our inner image of ourselves can always be improved. At the end of the day, it doesn't matter how many people give us compliments, it's the compliments we give ourselves that determine our long-term emotional wellbeing and our results.

You may well find this exercise challenging to start with. Your mind may be jumping all over the place or an image of you just will not come through. That's OK. Trust the process. The first few times you do anything is a challenge. Another side benefit is that this exercise is also strengthening your will, which is one of your mind's creative faculties, and will improve your level of focus, concentration and persistence in all other areas of your life.

There's no formula to follow when it comes to forming an image in your mind. What you see with your eyes closed will be unique to you. Success is personal. You may see yourself breezing through a tough conversation with your boss. What did you say? How did you stand? What expression was on your face? Where were your hands? What made you so assertive? What shoes were you wearing?

Maybe an image of you returning home to your loved ones who can't wait to see you appears. Where have you been? What colour shirt/dress/blouse are you wearing? What does your hair look like? Are you

Chapter 10: You Are One Act Away

smiling? What car are you driving? What deodorant do you smell of?

It could even be you in 20 years' time who's on the beach with your grandchildren.

Go with whatever comes to your mind when it's in flow and really play with your perception faculty. See yourself from the front, from the side, from the back. Get a full 360-degree view of who you are and mop up all those details. Soak up everything you see, think and feel from the images that flash up in your mind.

Once you've played with your imagination for ten minutes or so, it's time to open your eyes and…

**Write the script.**

**EXERCISE STAGE TWO: WRITE YOUR SCRIPT/** Writing the script is the fun part, and you don't have to be a renowned filmmaker and screenwriter like Steven Spielberg in order to do it because you're merely writing down everything you've just seen in your imagination. You're the only one who can write the script because you're the only one who has seen the person you want to become. Only you have access to the images you form in your mind.

There are two rules to your writing:

**RULE NUMBER 1** is that you write everything in the present tense as if it's happening right now. The reason you write in the present tense is because the idea is to plant this new image of yourself in your subconscious mind, and your subconscious mind has no concept of the past or future. It knows only the here and now, so writing in the present tense gets you speaking its language.

**RULE NUMBER 2** is that you only write about the positive aspects of the things that you want to bring into your life and never write about the negative things you want to get away from. The reason for this is that the subconscious mind does not register filler words and only moves the words of context and feeling into form. As you now understand, writing about things you want floods your consciousness with the ideals you want to move towards and impresses them upon the subconscious mind. However, this also works the other way around, so writing about the things you don't want will instead impress these on the subconscious mind and in doing so deliver you more of what you don't want.

**DON'T DO THIS**

To make it really clear for you, here's an example of a negative thing you may want to get away from that's written in the present tense:

"I've got no monthly car payments, overdraft and credit card debt."

Sounds great, doesn't it? No debt! But here's the catch – your subconscious only hears, "I've got monthly car payments, overdraft, credit card debt." Using this example, you're impressing the idea of monthly car payments, overdrafts and credit card debt upon your subconscious. Even though it's not your intention, it's what you are doing because that's what you're thinking about. You give energy to whatever you focus on.

When someone has a goal to get out of debt, often they'll stay in debt forever because debt is what they're thinking about.

**DO THIS INSTEAD**

Here's a positive thing you may want to move towards that's written in the present tense:

"I am financially independent because I invest money into cash-flowing assets that go up in value over time."

Your subconscious hears, "I am financially independent. I invest money into cash-flowing assets that go up in value over time." Do you notice how your feelings shift to a positive vibration when you read the statement? Can you see the difference? Even though the outcomes are the same from both statements (I have no debt), the way in which they're worded is very different and that is what leads to different results.

Choose your words very wisely when you're writing your own script!

## Here are some passages that I wrote from a couple of my visualisations…

*Ant Austen – the dad to Ryan*
*I'm a dependable dad to Ryan who is always nudging him into his best self so he can live a wonderful life of full and honest expression. My advice is compelling, advancing and always delivered as a suggestion rather than an instruction. My mission is to arm Ryan with the self-confidence to step out from the crowd and really bet on himself, so he thinks for himself and*

backs his own judgement. To see him listen to others, consider their ideas, but to make the final decision based on his own verdict. I teach him this by walking my talk so he's receiving a non-verbal message from me. This ranges from financial behaviours to everyday success habits that enrich my relationships, lifestyle and my wellbeing so that my message gets transferred to him.

*Ant Austen – the football player*
*I'm a top-class football player who always scores spectacular goals. I make the game look easy and move around the pitch with elegance. My ball control is deft, like the ball is landing on a bed of feathers when it touches my foot. Due to my radar vision through having a 360-degree awareness of the game, my touch direction always has me moving into space with the ball. This is how I retain possession of the ball for my team and is why I always have time on the ball. My passing is precise and fizzes into my teammate so they receive the ball with ease. My game intelligence is the best I've seen, which allows me to bring other players into play, create goal-scoring opportunities and to put myself in goal-scoring territory. Scoring goals is the easiest part of football for me. I'm the fittest player on the pitch, always, which means I can jump higher than my opponent to win headers, change direction faster and be stronger when shielding the ball.*

*Ant Austen – the author*
*My writing moves people to take actions that make a positive difference to their lives. My stories evoke emotion in my readers which they can't get enough of. My books are known as page-turners and are read over and over again. They are a huge talking point around the world where my words are examined and studied by satisfied, fascinated people who are driven to succeed in a big way. I just love writing, full stop. I love the craft and the ever-fulfilling promise of connection through and beyond life. I write to inspire, to give people ideas and success templates to follow, and to deepen my own understanding of who I am so I'm better equipped to help other people get what they want out of life.*

Notice how everything is written in the present tense as if it's happening now. I've described a "perfect world" character of how I want to be now. Notice how zero negatives are mentioned so only the positive aspects are being heard by my subconscious.

Once you've gotten to this stage, congratulations. You have essentially written your script. I should mention that I would argue that the script is never fully completed. The goal is to design the person you want to become in such precise detail that you'll keep refining it. It's my opinion that a good-natured person who acts out an ever-evolving script of continuous improvement will be a person who lives a fulfilled life; they'll be someone who ends up being pretty pleased with themselves in their later years because they adapted to the ever-changing world and recreated themselves where needed to still come out on top.

Now you've written your script, well done. You've given form to the person you want to be. You've broadened your awareness and you have given definition to the perfect world you that you derived from your imagination. Now, you not only have a solid baseline of the desired you to work with, you also have a written script to review and refine as you go.

*You're now ready to start acting like the person you want to become.*

### Act your way to success

Success is different for every person. It comes in various forms and definitions. You know that your script is your definition of success, but the question of whether success comes to you or not is entirely answered by and dependent on your actions.

For example, let's say you earn £30,000 per year and you want to earn £100,000 per year. Your first action is finding a role that pays £100,000 per year. The second action is calling the HR department. The third action is applying for the job. The fourth action is showing up to the interview. These all take place in the outside world.

Visualisation, positive thinking, prior planning and a belief re-evaluation gets you ready to receive £100,000, but these inside world things alone cannot make the £100,000 fall in your lap. Yes, they hook you up to a higher frequency and move the £100,000 towards you, but unless you move yourself towards it through action, you won't materialise the £100,000. To be blunt, positive thinking without positive action gets you positively nowhere.

I just want to reiterate this point to make it crystal clear for you. Forming pictures of you earning £100,000 in the non-physical world of your mind is an essential practice, but you cannot meditate, dream or wish yourself into a £100,000-a-year role on a physical level without taking action. There are simply things you have to do after you finish meditating to make it happen – like find a £100,000-a-year role, call HR, apply for the job and then show up to the interview.

So, that means the only way to move yourself from where you are today to where you want to be in the future is through action. Everything you have in your life right now is evidence of this, insomuch as the way you've been acting up until this point has brought you to what you have today. If you're not where you thought you'd be right now or you're not surrounded by the things you want, the harsh yet honest reason is because you've been taking the wrong action.

By this I mean that getting where you want to get to in the future requires you taking the right action from this moment forward. If you're now asking yourself, "What's the point in writing a script when action is the determining factor that brings about success?" the answer is simple – you write the script to ensure you're on the right track and to answer the following question…

### What is the right action?

Well, the right action for you is your right action. I can't tell you what your right action is because it's different from mine. Only you can define what your right action is by reviewing, acting out and updating your ever-evolving script.

What I can tell you is that there are far too many good-natured people in the world taking the wrong action. They're working themselves to the bone in a quest to make a good living, but they're not really living at all because they feel trapped, short on time and financially stunted.

They feel beaten down and hard done by because they followed the well-known template for life to a tee. Go to school, get good grades, get a good job and live a good life. You could argue that this is the outline of someone else's script.

Acting without your own script means acting without deliberate cause and this leads to an unknown effect, much like working a week's trial at a job without knowing what the role pays leads to an unknown paycheque.

In fact, acting without the right cause guarantees to bring the wrong effect. For example, solely lifting weights in the gym is not the right cause to affect weight loss, because lifting weights is a cause to affect muscle mass and weight gain.

Back when my belief about having to work longer hours than the average person to be successful was in full swing, I'd get an idea and move straight into action like a headless chicken. Despite my desire, persistence and faith, I'd always fall short because I had no real definitive goal to act on and move towards.

### Here's how that went…

As a child, I had a burning desire to be a professional football player who played for Tottenham Hotspur.

I admired skilful players like Paul Gascoigne and David Ginola who could do things with a football that had never been seen before. They were exciting to watch because they were unpredictable. When they got the ball, you felt like you were about to witness some magic. I wanted to play football just like them.

I remember practising my football skills in a certain way so I could glide through a barrage of opposing players with flair and elegance. Through repetition, I developed high technical skill with the ball that gave me the ability to shimmy out of tight areas and create goal-scoring chances for my team. I consistently did it in training, small-

## Chapter 10: You Are One Act Away

sided games and friendly matches. Yet when it came to crunch time, the big games, I'd go missing. I'd tense up. I'd withdraw into myself and be a shadow of the player I and everyone else knew I was.

This issue did not come down to the personal action I was taking. If I heard another player was in the gym five times a week, I was in the gym six times a week. If I heard a player could kick the ball on to the crossbar in three kicks, I'd train myself to do it in two. A lack of action on my part wasn't the issue. I was a hard worker and no one was ever going to outwork me.

It took years of frustration trying to figure out what was going wrong. For a long time, I put it down to just not being good enough at football. But deep down, I knew that wasn't true and the warrior in me wasn't willing to accept it.

What I eventually figured out was that my idea of how I should play in competitive football matches was different to how I performed in training games. A football match is two opposing teams battling it out in a win/lose scenario whereas a training game comes with no real consequence – two very different situations. Practising my skills in the garden and using them in training was fine, but my subconscious belief was that using them in a football match was high risk, so I wouldn't try things. In essence, I wasn't expressing myself when I played competitively.

I had defined how to perform in training games, but I had not defined how to perform in the football matches that mattered and would move me towards my goal of being a professional footballer. As a result, I'd flip from being a fearless beast in training to a frightened rabbit on match-days. There's no doubt pressure and my belief system played a part, but the main reason I struggled was that I had no real definition to work towards, no script to act out.

In the same way that going to school to get good grades, to get a good job and live a good life is a vague idea, my idea of being a professional football player was left to chance because I did not define the type of person I had to become in order to be a professional footballer.

Despite never reaching my own potential as a footballer, football is not a sour subject for me because it's been my greatest teacher. It taught me that in order to do something, you first have to be something. The person I had to be to shine in football matches was not the same person who could shine so brightly in training.

At the time of writing this book in 2023, I'm playing my football in an over-35s team. While some would argue my best playing years are past me, and despite having no attached anterior cruciate ligament in my left knee, I'm defying the odds and playing some of the best football I've ever played. Why now? Because I've written the script and I'm acting the part.

If you're thinking, "Oh, but that's all right for you, you're naturally gifted at football," think again.

*Don't get hung up on the myth that natural ability is required in order to excel at something.*

Personally, I don't believe natural ability is a thing. I feel it's often cited by envious people to deliberately disregard the persistent action that most people are unwilling to take to win.

Retired Jamaican sprinter Usain Bolt was not the fastest runner of all time when he was born in 1986. His future running ability stemmed from the daily action he took to move himself towards the idea of being a world record holder.

In 2001, he won a silver medal in the high school championships' 200m sprint, with a time of 22.04 seconds. In 2009 he ran the distance in 19.19 seconds and set a new 200m sprint world record. Notice that his success did not happen overnight, but the important point to note is that it did happen.

How? Because he stuck with his idea and took persistent action. The right action.

Usain Bolt being a world record holder of the 100m sprint, 200m sprint and 4 × 100m relay is not down to natural ability or luck – unless luck means **L**abouring **U**nder **C**orrect **K**nowledge (remember that from Chapter 1?).

Chapter 10: You Are One Act Away

When you take an idea, define it and take the right action, there really is no limit to what you can achieve.

## Embody the part you want to play

Take Austin Butler, the actor who played Elvis Presley in the 2022 box office hit movie *Elvis* – a pretty daunting role and very big shoes to fill. Perhaps even more so when you hear comments like those shared by jazz and soul singer Michael Bublé, who said in an interview that the reason Elvis could sing the way he did was because, "God had kissed his voice."

In preparation for the role, Austin Butler watched every film Elvis made, every documentary about him and even went to Elvis' house and sat in one of the rooms, called the Jungle Room, to play the guitar and sing Elvis songs.

Every day for two years, Austin Butler acted like Elvis Presley. To mimic the way Elvis walked, talked and sang is one thing; to understand his upbringing and act from his beliefs, values, and profession is quite another. However, this was the method that led to Austin Butler winning a Golden Globe and BAFTA Award for his performance.

Stood on the red carpet after the movie premiere were Elvis' ex-wife Priscilla Presley and his best friend Jerry Schilling. When asked what they thought of Austin Butler's portrayal, they said that during certain points of the film, they kept looking at each other because they could not work out if they were still watching Austin or Elvis himself had been cut into the scene.

Fancy that. Even Elvis' family and friends could mistake someone else for the King of Rock 'n' Roll. What's more, a stream of professional singers have said that no one will ever come close to singing like Elvis Presley, and yet Austin Butler, an actor who's not a singer but who knows how to act in a certain way, can sing just like him. How did Austin Butler achieve what many considered impossible? By visualising the character in the script so completely that he came to embody that character, even if only for the duration of shooting the movie.

The point I'm trying to make is that if you follow what all the great actors do, you can become a modified character of yourself and live the life you truly want to live. You can use your imagination to see yourself as you want to see yourself, and then you can start acting like that and become that person.

You may not want to sing like Elvis Presley, run like Usain Bolt or play football like Paul Gascoigne, but what do you want to do? More importantly, who do you have to be in order to do it?

Before you can **do** something, you first must **be** something.

Ultimately, success comes from action and by acting in a certain way. Thinking in a certain way is the starting point but it will not get the job done. Only by action can you improve yourself and your results.

At the end of the day, you get what you are. So what do you have to do and who do you have to be on a daily basis to have what you want to have?

I'm not saying you have to turn into Elvis or a superhero, but I'm sure you're aware that in order to have something different, you're going to have to act differently. As the saying goes, "If you always do what you've always done, you'll always have what you've always had." If you aren't feeling fulfilled in the life you currently live, what can you do differently to start turning the ship in a new direction?

Of course, where you are mentally is what will give you the direction you need in order to steer your "ship". To that end, it's worth remembering that there are only three places you can mentally spend your time: the past, the present and the future.

### Strike the right balance

While you can choose to spend your time mentally in one of these three places, it's important to find the right balance between examining your past, living in your present and visualising your future.

## Chapter 10: You Are One Act Away

The past is there to remind us of what's happened in life. It's there to inform us, but much like the profit and loss report in business, it's a report that comes too late. At the end of the day, the past is the past, and there's absolutely nothing you can do to change it. It's gone. People who mentally live in the past magnify their feelings of the same situations and validate their beliefs.

All too often, we focus on the bad parts of our past – the ones where we felt negative emotions. This is what we dwell on. If you find yourself frequently raking over what's been and gone, I suggest you start using your creative faculties to transport yourself to your most beautiful moments and feel those feelings again. Saturate yourself in them and intensify them until you feel them surge through every cell of your body, as though these feelings are beaming out of your fingertips. Use the past as the reminder it is, but don't live there, and if you must magnify your past, submerge yourself in the positive feelings, rather than the negative.

This will make you feel electric in the present. Of course, living in the moment is the buzzword of modern culture – I'll also jump on the bandwagon, so I'm suggesting you spend 80 per cent of your time here to ensure you take actions that make a difference in the present moment. You're in full control in the present – you are time, remember.

The present moment is the only thing you truly own. How you act, look and feel in the present moment is you as the master at work, and you must be the master. You're not here to let life pull you around every second of the day. Life gets its fair share of pushing us around against our will as it is.

But to have true power in the present, you also need to dedicate time to developing hope in your future. The way to have hope in the future is by designing your future well. By taking action in the present to work out what you want, you can write goals down and make a progressive realisation towards your worthy ideal.

Your worthy ideal is a future ideal. Now, some people make the mistake of living permanently in the future. These people never get anything done. They're too busy talking about what they're going to do one day, but they never take action in the present and so "one day" never becomes "today".

These people are often labelled delusional because they wish for it all to fall in their lap.

You want to spend 20 per cent of your time constructing your future and going through it in your mind. Like I said, hope in the future gives you power in the present, so it's important to spend a percentage of our time on future orientation. All successful people are future-pacing their identity. They're saying things like, "I am an entrepreneur and property investor," even though they're currently an employee and renting an apartment. They are setting goals to move themselves closer to this worthy ideal and, in doing so, they are creating the space they need to grow into their future.

So, you should always ask yourself if you've given yourself enough space to grow. Setting sales goals in business is creating space. Opening a new bank account is creating space. Setting goals is a simple way for you to create more space to grow into.

## Balance intention with attention

Just as we have to balance our past, present and future in our minds, we also have to balance our intention with attention when it comes to the physical actions we take. With too much intention, you'll spend all your time planning, setting goals and talking/thinking about what you're going to do. 100 per cent intention slides you into a worse place than you started because you never take action or get anything done.

With too much attention, on the other hand, you put your head down and get to work. You've set no intention, which means you have no goals, no plans, no thought. Most people are like this because they were brought up on the belief, "Hard work alone brings success." But you and I know that's not true – just as complete intention holds you back from making progress, 100 per cent attention brings the risk of you working on the wrong plan your entire life because you never looked up. You might be making progress, but you could be moving left when really you want to move right.

The ideal to shoot for is 20 per cent intention and 80 per cent attention. Intention always comes first because the clearer you are on the outcome, the easier it is to run a plan to get to the outcome. When you have the outcome and the plan, you can focus your attention on acting in the specific way that lines up with the intention you set. You can embody the person you want to become and, in doing so, move yourself towards your ideal life.

The title of this chapter – You Are One Act Away – says it all; you just need to take one action in the right direction to start moving. The more right actions you take, the more quickly you will progress towards your worthy ideal.

Your actions now you've finished reading this book could be starting with just one of the success habits I've identified. Just think, if you introduced one of these habits into your life every two weeks, then within less than six months you could be living a happier life, one that is much more aligned with your vision of ideal.

**ONE ACT AWAY SUCCESS HABIT/** Take the vision of your ideal life that you've created and start acting as though you're already there. Take action to start moving towards the elements of your worthy ideal that aren't yet within your grasp. Be intentional about the actions you take in the present to bring you closer to the future you desire.

I can take no credit for all that you achieve after finishing this book because, as you know, everything you want and desire comes from within *you*. All I've done by sharing my learnings and journey is open the door and show you that, if you take that act of stepping through, you'll find a whole new world on the other side.

**At the end of the day, your wants, desires and dreams are unique to you. So, you need to know exactly who you are if you want to bring those wants, desires and dreams into your life.**

# CONCLUSION

Thank you for reading this book. I sincerely hope you're seeing yourself in a much brighter light than before you read this book. I hope you're vividly aware of your awesome power to change and you're firmly convinced you already have everything you need to live a purposeful life by design. All in all, I hope you have a new-found sense of confidence in your abilities and you're totally at home in your own skin.

Never would I tell you how to live your life. I'm just keen to throw ideas at you because I know that you're a creator who can create an amazing life for yourself. I want my words to spark new ideas in your own mind that lead to you living a happy, healthy and wealthy life.

The big idea I've been trying to impress on you throughout this book is that success comes from inside. At the end of each day, you're only going to be left with you – regardless of what you accomplish. When you're lying in bed with your eyes closed, unable to escape your thoughts and your feelings, it's important that you're feeling good so you can get a good night's sleep and wake up feeling good.

By the way, use this time to raise your vibration. Think back through your day and mentally say thank you for all the good things that happened so you drift off to sleep in a positive vibration.

I encourage you to have fun and go all in on life because I believe life should be enjoyed. You only get one shot at it. So when you're approaching the end of the road, and you're resting your eyes and well-used body like the droves of elderly people sitting in armchairs of care homes, you can relive your wonderful life all over again in your mind.

Let's round up this book by briefly going through what I've shared with you…

***You are limitless*** – An endless supply of thoughts, ideas and suggestions are forever flowing into your mind. The flow cannot be switched off, but you can bring order to the flow by bringing order to your mind.

In the same way you can build dreams, ideals and chosen fantasies in your mind, you also have the ability to build a physical replica of those same things in the outside world. You can do this because you possess the same creative faculties that have created every material thing you see in the outside world. Creative faculties that remain limitless and are not measurable because they have not yet been beaten.

*You are time* – Time is something you're only conscious of because you exist. Without you, you would have no concept of time. Which means if you're not getting vital things done, it's not due to a lack of time, it's down to you. You do all the things you do each day because they're what you deem to be the most important things to get done. It's therefore worth finding out whether you're spending or investing time in the right places by doing the things you choose to do.

*You are electric* – You're living in a body that vibrates in accordance with the domineering thought impulses of your mind. If you think good, you feel good. If you think bad, you feel bad. The rate of your vibration determines what you receive from life because you can only attract to you that which is vibrating in harmony with you. When you know how to change your state and you're consciously aware of the vibration you're in, you also know how to make yourself vibrate in harmony with the good that you desire so you can attract it.

*You are subconscious* – You're always the absolute expression of the current ideas that have flowered in your subconscious mind. The reason why new ideas excite you in principle and scare you in reality is because your subconscious has not yet accepted the new idea. Its primary job is to keep you alive so it will urge you with all of its might to step back into safety instead of forward into growth. Your subconscious remains in charge. Thankfully, through repetition, you can reprogram it to charge you forward towards your worthy ideals.

*You are habitual* – Habits die hard. And you have hundreds of habits. You're doing loads of things on a daily basis without giving any conscious thought to them. Since it's ultimately the things we do that either keep us stuck in a rut or bring us success, the trick is to replace your bad habits with good habits so you end up stuck with them. Just imagine how successful you'll be when you don't have to give any conscious thought to being happy, grateful and productive.

*You are unbelievable* – In a literal sense, your creative faculties make you unbelievable. Also, you have the ability to restructure your entire belief system so it's working with you rather than against you. You can unbelieve all of the beliefs that limit you and direct all of your emotion into positive energy by believing new beliefs that line up with the good that you desire.

*You are insensitive* – Getting your message across to a group of people or getting your voice heard is a challenge that we all face on a daily basis. Since people generally build strong and instant bonds with the people they have things in common with, you can create deeper connections with other people by talking to them on their level. This will enable you to be a strong leader in business, a more rounded parent or spouse at home and a better friend to your friends. But before you can reap any of the benefits that come from communicating better, you must first know your own communication style.

*You are blessed* – You don't have to look very far to find that your life is already full of wonderful things. Gratitude is the fastest way to raise your vibration. By giving thanks for everything you do have, you're putting yourself on the frequency to receive more of what you're thankful for. Gratitude is a multiplier of all great things.

*You are under construction* – No matter how well you do in life, you're always going to be raising the bar for yourself because the spiritual side of your personality is forever seeking expansion and fuller expression. This is why we want certain things. The reason why our wants are personal to us is because our wants come from the essence of who we are. Once you're in the habit of bringing order to the endless flow of thoughts, ideas and suggestions coming into your mind, you're always going to be inspired to unveil more of your greatness.

*You are one act away* – All you really need to do is act the part. You need to act like the person you want to become so the things you want will naturally come to you. As the saying goes, before you can *have* something, you first must *be* something. When you don't know who you are, you have no character reference and no script to act out.

**So, who the hell are you?**

# ABOUT THE AUTHOR

Ant Austen is the founder of BeTheLimitlessYou, a personal development company, who believes the fundamental principle to living a purposeful life comes through a person understanding who they are. Driven to help others, Ant spends his time writing, reading and studying so he can broaden the awareness of ambitious people and teach them something about themselves. He believes that a person must understand who they are so they can discard all of the things they tolerate and don't serve them with confidence, and so they can start living in a way that lines up with their purpose.

Ant started out in business at the age of 23 and has been a business owner ever since. He also plays football, invests in property and lives in Guernsey with his wife, son and daughter.

Printed in Dunstable, United Kingdom